# M·O·D·E·R·N  T·I·M·E·S

Peter York has given the decade many of
its favourite names and buzz words —
from Mayfair Mercenaries to
Reactionary Chic. *Modern Times* is his
fifth book. His first, *Style Wars,*
described the social worlds of the late
seventies; the three that followed —
the best-selling *Sloane Rangers'* trilogy
(co-authored with Anne Barr)
described the enclosed world of one
group of people with deadly accuracy.

Style editor of *Harpers and Queen,* Peter
York is also a contributing editor of
*Vanity Fair* in the USA. In 1983 he
wrote and presented *Hey Good Looking,*
a complete five-part series on style and
its meaning, for Channel Four. A
regular contributor to other television
programmes like *The Tube* and
*Saturday Review,* he is currently
working on a major documentary
series on British Youth culture.

Apart from his writing, Peter York is a
founding partner in a group of
business consultancy companies which
advise businesses and institutions here
and overseas.

# M·O·D·E·R·N

# T·I·M·E·S

## Peter York

Futura

_IL69916_

A Futura Book

Copyright © Peter York 1984

First published in Great Britain in 1984
by William Heinemann Ltd, London W1

This editon published in 1985 by
Futura Publications, a Division of
Macdonald & Co (Publishers) Ltd
London & Sydney

ISBN 0 7088 2718 7

Printed in Great Britain by
Billing & Sons Ltd., Worcester

Futura Publications
A Division of
Macdonald & Co (Publishers) Ltd
Maxwell House
74 Worship Street
London EC2A 2EN

A BPCC plc Company

# ACKNOWLEDGEMENTS

My thanks to:

*Harry Green* for getting the point and
   putting it across so smartly in the
   design of the book
*Mira Connolly* for her diligent and high-
   speed picture research
*David Godwin* for commissioning the
   book in the first place
*Diana Avebury* who introduced us
*Ros Edwards* for pulling the whole
   thing together
*Kate Gardiner* for production
*Sally Gough* for dealing with the
   actual words
*Lynne Hunt* who put a lot straight
*Anne Barr* and *Willie Landels* of
   *Harpers & Queen* for my 'editor
   without portfolio' job and all
   their support
*Tina Brown* for commissioning *The
   Voice*, *The Glint* and *Not Shaving* for
   *Vanity Fair*
*Lendal Scott-Ellis* who contributed a lot
   to those pieces
*Parke Puterbaugh* who commissioned
   *How the Wedge Was Won* for *Rolling
   Stone*
*Kim Evans* who produced and directed
   *Hey Good Looking* so sharply
*Melvyn Bragg* and *Nick Evans* who
   watched over *Hey Good Looking* and
   allowed it to happen
*Mark Holloway* who disinterred
   wonderful archive for *HGL*
*Robert Elms* who talked clubland
   history
*Alexandra Artley* and *Gavin Stamp* for
   their clever and witty chronology of
   re-Victorianisation in *Victorian
   Values*

Peter York

# C·O·N·T·E·N·T·S

H·E·Y   G·O·O·D

L·O·O·K·I·N·G

# S·T·Y·L·E

*Style* is the way things look and the way they are. Oscar Wilde, who got some things right, said: 'Only fools don't judge by appearances.' Appearances ... manner, the way you say, that's him, that's her, that's one of them. Style, it's the most difficult word in the language.

First, let's ask why people go on so much about *style* now.

There always was a thing called *fashion*, and if you had enough money you could always dress up in it. But style was something different, unquestioned. In the old world people didn't go on about style because they *knew their place*.

Compared with us, people in the past lived in the dark, in a style prison. Most days they didn't see any *pictures* of things at all. They lived completely within their own world. The church was the only movie house. Rich men had castles, poor people hung around the gates. Even a gentleman was a pretty well-defined thing.

If you'd been a groom in the royal stables and you'd dressed up like the king, you'd have been put away for it. You'd have been a pretender or a madman.

Style was clearly different from fashion. Style was – the way you were. Style was just the way your kind of people were. It just *was*.

But it's different now. People have forgotten their place. Since the war people in the West have had more and more of everything. It started with just useful things. A refrigerator, a car.

Then it got on to media and holidays and experiences and having an interesting time and eventually learning to be an interesting person.

As people's lives became more interesting, as

they did more, and went on more holidays and courses and sport sessions, and ate more foreign food, they were keener to change the style that had been handed down to them by previous generations.

They wanted to be seen as interesting people with interesting clothes, opinions and attitudes, whose choice reflected their own fascinating and inimitable personalities. Their *individual* style as they wanted to see it.

In America they've already got to this stage called self-expression and they've taken it a bit far, there they have books saying you can do anything, like live for ever.

Argyll style: who says the art of conversation's dead when a man can make a point with his socks?

still or moving – in the history of the world. It's all there in living colour. Infinite choice.

This way lies madness of course. And the freer people became, free of God and tedious rules and constraints, the more lots and lots of people in the West were *liberated* – remember that word – free from taboos and conventions, from other people's expectations, from family and background, the more they cast their eyes, fascinated, on other people whose style was as far removed from their own as possible.

These people took the hard realities that they'd seen beautified in the colour supplements and made them into fashion.

The bland and liberated middle classes wanted to see more and more pictures of people whose lifestyles really *were* extreme.

They feel there isn't enough flavour in their lives now that everything that's bad for them has been removed. Not enough style – the terrible conundrum.

Style has become the added ingredient that people started to get *by sharing other people's lives.*

So – if you want to find a style that suits you – come down to the style vault. The whole world, past and present, is your dressing-up box. Now you use your style to express not just who you are, but who you'd *like* to be.

Democracy means everyone can have a style and style's become the new language. Who says the art of conversation's dead when a man can make a point with his socks?

So you see, once you understand the language, it's OK to judge by appearances.

Tom Wolfe described this in his brilliant essay *The "Me" Decade.*

By 1980 the old world and the new didn't exist side by side – they'd cross-bred. Lifestyles were up for rent. No one quite knew what the rules were any more – it was all very confusing. Fashion cut across the old social orders of style.

Now you can have magazine articles actually encouraging you to dress in royal style, or gent's style, there's no law against it. No rules or commonsense about clothes.

And the vocabulary of style you can use is huge because there are so many pictures around, there've never been so many pictures – old, new,

STYLE

# F·A·S·H·I·O·N

In a time gone by what people now call style was then called fashion, and fashion had to be followed.

Fashion had its own establishment, a kind of Vatican, in the fifties and sixties and in this set-up they had dictators who set the lines for everybody to follow.

The lines were set like edicts in the way of the old world.

These rules were simple, broadly *de haut en bas*, i.e. set by the visible rich for poorer people – the deferentials – who wanted to copy them. And by older – 25-plus established people – for younger ones. 'Kids' – teenagers – in the fifties wanted to look more adult and sophisticated. And fashions were set at the centre, meaning Paris, France and filtered across – and *down* as they saw it then – to Bradford, England.

They were set by magazine editors for magazine readers. *Vogue* used to announce the colour of the season and up and down the land shops presented clothes in banana beige or coral red or whatever.

In the fifties there were actually *lines* for fashion. Dictates about the shape a woman's clothes should be, irrespective of the shape of her. And then came the sixties. Remember the mini . . .

And the point was that everyone wore it, your sister, your auntie, the gym mistress, everyone.

For truly THERE WAS NO ALTERNATIVE. You were either with them or against them. It was, to use a word the social-worker type of person favours, very authoritarian.

This imperial phase in the history of style lasted from the beginning of mass high-street fashion in the fifties until the late sixties when people did all

sorts of funny things in the name of freedom. They grew discontented with the set menu of fashion. The problem was the great God, 'Me', whose voice was heard everywhere.

But it was hard for women – and for men – to follow 'Me' if thay had the stamp of the great God *Vogue* on their backs as clear as a McAlpine donkey jacket.

People began to say, 'I made this up myself. I'm a terrific artistic and creative type of person and I've made myself into a work of art.'

So, in the early seventies the Paris, France monolith fell.

It fell because people were beginning to want clothes that said a bit more than . . . I've just been to Chelsea Girl, or Chelsea Boy, and spent 29/11.

This idea of individuality and self-expression worked against the central theme of one-dimensional, mass young fashion with chains in every high street. Some lost their touch, didn't adapt fast enough to this new lust for choice. They closed.

The response was variety under the same roof, fashion shopping malls, bazaars of fast fashion, like Kensington Market, with air-conditioning.

In these new temples, at first, predictably, they just copied what individuals did. Individual fashion was called, oddly enough, street fashion, as if the other kind was never worn in the street.

The fashion zoo. Ethnic look safely behind Graphic bars in South Molton street provides conversation point

And then they rushed to get it into the shops, on the dummies, before it went out of style.

*This was a mistake.* It was a mistake because it was a risk. They thought that if they just took the line from newer younger *street* people full of modern hormones, they'd still be able to call the tune. Sometimes they struck lucky and hit on looks which sold. But more often, they got it wrong, and their whole world-view seemed to fall apart.

And, anyway, in their secret heart of hearts the little consumers still wanted something to belong to.

The fashion industry started producing wavelets of new styles *stolen* from all over the place. Fantasies, so you could try other people's lives on for size. Instead of *lines* they had *looks* now. Here are some of them:

– The sporting type of person look which was a mixture of *Chariots of Fire* and the kids from *Fame*, but had very little to do with exercise.

– The classy look, which showed you understood the difference between red wine and Horlicks and could probably get on a horse.

– The ethnic look, which showed your sympathies with the Third World. And this gave another dimension to your interesting personality.

– The nostalgic look, which showed that you'd watched *Brideshead Revisited* and still kept in touch with your teddy bear.

At the end of the seventies, as times got harder, kids wanted to look smarter, sharper, richer, less depressed. They were keener to follow the rules again – if they could work out which ones to follow.

Because by then there was a distinct problem – not knowing where the rules were in a time when *your parents* had just taken up the idea of anything goes. Breaking the rules and following them, both proved difficult. Kids will emerge not knowing which rules to break because they'll have grown up not knowing what they were in the first place.

Intelligent kids began to worry that they'd be stuck for ever with the terrifying old-fashioned notion of continuous innovation. Having to ask themselves every morning, 'Who am I going to be today?'

I've always said creativity ends in tears.

The only answer was to reinvent the rules and pretend you believed in them. It gives a meaning to life.

Army surplus, for instance, is a recurring fashion factor. This time round, the Falklands was a great help. Uniform, sir? Fan-bloody-tastic. I mean, how original. This kind of reactionary chic could solve the problem. It could set everything to rights because, in the end, everyone wants a nice uniform even more than they want self-expression.

That's why . . . a certain kind of person feels so at home in stripes, so safe in shades, so grateful for grey, so fun in fifties, so brave in black.

Join the Culture Club.

Everyone knows politics is about performance when it's on TV, and nowadays that's how viewers award their points and their votes. Everyone judges politicians by how they put themselves across – by their style.

It helps to think of the House of Commons as a kind of nineteenth-century theatre tricked up as a

# P·O·L·I·T·I·C·A·L
# S·T·Y·L·E

Gothic palace. Better still, think of it as a kind of *museum* of style, because political styles are extreme, theatrical and, in this country, they're deliberately archaic. The House of Commons lives in the 1940s, go and look at it. But it *dreams* of the 1830s.

Politicians were always very style conscious. They've got to project, just like actors. And they don't just project their own background, they've got to project their area, their party and the style of the people they want to vote for them.

You come to recognise some distinct political looks. Some of them haven't changed much. There's the Nonconformist patriach look now worn by Rhodes Boyson. You can see him running a Victorian academy for the Improving Classes, just like his predecessor probably did. Edward Heath's a rather more up-to-date model for Westminster – the Euro-Tory. Everything about him says *modern* and professional – in a slightly old-fashioned sixties way. Then there's the *traditional* Labour MP style, Roy Mason, the genial mining MP in his Sunday suit and Rugby League tie – early Burtons. And there's the new centre – the Volvo people – Liberals and SDP. They're a bit trendy in their way, a bit enlightened and co-ordinated, rather like Horne Brothers leisurewear. And I imagine they help with the washing-up.

TV changed everything. In the fifties and sixties politicians had to learn how to appeal to everyone

Edwardian SuperMac look,
modelled by Harold Macmillan
with a few flyaway buttons

Gatsby President, John F. Kennedy,
and Jackie step out
into the sixties

POLITICAL STYLE

– close up. If you didn't play the media game you didn't get on. Michael Foot decided to remain part of the pre-TV age, and look what happened. He looks what he is – the corduroy, the wool tie, the academic's white hair – he could be a radical clergyman or an old-style professor of architecture who believed in truth to materials. He's a product of the thirties, a Hampstead intellectual, an early CND man.

Tony Benn started off doing what the Press wanted. In the 1960s he was a nice-looking, modern, telegenic type. All white-hot progress and technology. The kind of upper-middle-class person who says they're classless. Woooh! He doesn't look the same now. Now he just says what he believes in and looks distinctly Old Testament. And some people find that hard going.

Harold Macmillan was the first TV Prime Minister. He loved it. He paced his speeches and his gestures for the cameras. He was a born actor. He was actually the first TV nostalgia act. A forerunner of *Upstairs Downstairs. He knew he was doing it*. Macmillan's great trick was to act as if he wasn't part of the TV age at all, as if he was an Edwardian gent. His droopy moustache and throwaway quips completed the impression of a toff who doesn't need to try too hard. But watch your back. Of course foreigners loved it. It's not surprising that J. F. Kennedy, the most media-conscious of presidents, became one of Super Mac's big buddies. He liked his style. Macmillan turned the trick by making the traditional Tory into a TV personality.

Harold Wilson camped up another style for the cameras. He was the suburban little man who pretends to be one of the boys. The friendly bank manager in the cupboard. It was all very homely and relaxed. But Harold Wilson wasn't really working-class at all. He just knew what image was wanted. He enjoyed using the right props. He projected a vision of the working-class past that was just like one of those Hovis commercials. It wasn't real, but it sold well, at the time.

*This* Prime Minister of course has changed everything. She's brought overt style out of the closet. Made it acceptable because she's a woman. To grow into her role as a leader of men she had,

*Left* Roy Mason, Miners' Union Labour
MP for Barnsley Central

*Right* Down-home caring check-shirt brand-
new denim 501 leisure-suit President,
Jimmy Carter

*Below left* Ken Livingstone for the Better
Badges party wears his heart on his lapel
plus Bohemian corduroy jacket, thoughtful
turtleneck, modern jazz hair and a
moustache of wide sympathies

*Below* Mrs Thatcher by Norman Parkinson:
a suit and tie for work. Early power-
dressing

however, to turn to a power symbol – the warrior queen. The Russians, obviously fans, gave her the clue with the 'Iron Lady' phrase and it's all gone like a dream ever since. These are different times from the sixties and Mrs Thatcher doesn't pretend to be the common person like Harold Wilson did. She emphasises her difference with all the symbolic trappings of office. She wears career lady suits with lapels and those bows and cravats which are a kind of pretend tie. Her hair is lacquered into Britannia's golden helmet, her voice is stronger, slower, deeper. She looks good in a different way now after the changes in make-up and teeth and so on. It all shows she's in control of herself. And people like the artifice. I think Margaret Thatcher mastered the nation by style, by projecting strength and certainty when the people wanted it. You can't argue with that rationally. When critics attack her, ordinary people say – just look at the opposition. They just don't look the part.

You can't ignore it. You can't pretend that style doesn't matter. Because every picture sells a Tory or a Socialist, or a militant tendency, and whoever masters the style game seems to win. We're stuck with it, that's what we give out points for, the performance, the production values: we know the actual job's done by machines.

POLITICAL STYLE

# E·X·E·C·U·T·I·V·E    S·T·Y·L·E

This is the story of the rise and decline of a whole style of person in just twenty-five years. Someone called the Executive.

The Executive rode the starship Free Enterprise from the fifties to the seventies. Just think – only the day before yesterday. The Executive Age was a time when a new look came along and summed up, *symbolised*, a whole lot of real social trends and gave them a name. It represented a revolution in business and in the way businessmen thought about themselves.

Do you remember in the sixties and early seventies the word executive was all over the place? Executive clothes, executive briefcases, executive cars, executive jets, executive washrooms, executive clubs, executive toys. It was even a brand name – the Ford Executive. The car for the man in the grey flannel suit. But looking at what's happening now, I suspect in a hundred years' time the only place you'll see the word executive will be in the dictionary. The executive style came out of this type of Fifties Modern business. And it was part of a new religion called management.

The roots of the executive style are in a building like the United Nations in New York. What this kind of building stands for is the idea of a new technology – cool and shiny and full of glass. Without fidgety columns or other homage to the past. It also stands for bureaucracy. Lots of smart bees in their departments and offices in a big glass hive all lit up and showing off.

The heart of the executive style is the multinational company. The stateless company that belongs everywhere. In the fifties and sixties these

HEY GOOD LOOKING

companies were proud of themselves, their size and their modernity, and they wanted to show it off. The early multi-nationals were *very* big, very international. Everyone looked busy and important – though you couldn't tell what they were doing. All the differences were kind of smoothed over. They were all international office people. Super Civil Servants. They had a style of their own. It was the style of a great institution and in the fifties, all sorts of businesses wanted to have that mystique. The style was very *professional*. Their key symbol was the computer and it's no coincidence that top hitmen always adopt the executive style.

So the executive look developed and it said modern, international, busy and professional. Executives aimed to look American-International even if they were working in Carlisle. It meant a dress code. Any colour as long as it was grey. The executive suit was a sleek boxy number in lightweight classless grey polyester worsted that was easy to pack and clean for air travel. The executive shoe was the new sixties slip-on. Light, modern, sleek. Executive briefcases were the equivalent of modern design in furniture – simple, functional, showing off new materials.

But it was more than just jobs and clothes, and architecture. There was a whole executive lifestyle based on the executive priorities. Control, communication, travel. Executives were supposed to be very scientific and numerate so of course they always liked any kind of electronic business machines – especially the ones that looked as though you controlled the world because they lit up and did sums. Of course, the Executive always had his calculator with *all the functions* on him at all times.

Being an Executive meant there was all that communicating to do. Executives had to communicate. They had to be involved in the exciting world of communications. Executive meant – always being in touch. Always informed. Special telephones, paging machines, Fax, satellites, telephone answering machines, car telephones, the lot. You can reach me on . . .

And Executive style was all about travel. All the ideal men in films and ads were always getting into flash cars, when they weren't climbing into jet planes – which were glamorous then. Executive travel meant *perks*. Living a bit of borrowed James Bondery on the company. Going Club Class because you were special; a seasoned traveller who needed the comfort to get all the work done. Then you'd be able to impress the board members at the other end. And being an Executive meant you paid for everything with Amex or Diners Club. Credit cards were really central to the executive imagery because they were international, they were computer-based and they were on firm. Executives liked collecting credit cards in special folders and discreetly flashing them around because the more you got the more your firm was prepared to pay for. They were executives' own little medals.

But they began to oversell the executive style – this was a mistake. They said that anyone could be an executive. And, of course, once you could buy the style ready-made, it stopped being glamorous.

The mid-seventies was the end of the executive empire. Everything smooth and bland and international suddenly seemed to fall apart. Once the modern world had actually happened, and really was everywhere, the executive style started to go . . . a little . . . how shall we put it . . . *down market*. It began to look a bit dated. If the world really was modern there was no need for it to look it. We were ready for The Past again.

The Executive style isn't exciting here any more. And – a bad sign – it's starting to look rather quaint and sixties to some young stylists. A bit funny. Lads like the Heaven 17s – awfully clever and Conceptual really – are already starting to muck about with the Executive Style, tongue in cheek, just as if it was as period and as far away as the Jazz Age.

And as the multi-nationals fold up and leave the cities, the lights twinkle in the last of the great office blocks and the last Executives fly off into the sunset. You can hear the little style historians sharpening their pencils, waiting to set the seal on another age. Baroque, Neo-classic, Romantic, *Executive*.

# R·E·A·C·T·I·O·N·A·R·Y
## C·H·I·C

*Laura Ashley
puts her weight
behind the
Austrian blind movement
in approximately
Onslow Square, SW7*

*Guilt-free
jeunesse doré*

### 1977

A wing-collar; a proper one, of course, heavy and stiff and a narrowish bow-tie, plus all this lounging and very considered behaviour. How very ... *Brideshead Revisited*. They must be reading it again.

### 1977 again

The 'visual jokes' have gone – didn't they have a bell-hop Thirties cut-out by the door, a Gospel Oaks Deco ziggurat by the windows and one of those sofas with sunray pleating? Now it's all marbled and stencilled in panels, with an Edwardian classical mahogany door under a pediment. And my God, this is a proper cocktail party – waiters and all – even if he did go to art school.

### 1978: a private view

*It is* Alex. What's he doing? (Greased hair, dark blue suit, very white Sea Island shirt, grey silk tie.) 'It's called Argentinian millionaire,' he says. It's a *look*, but he's just been to Buenos Aires and they're fabulously rich and glamorous. And horrible too? He says, 'You've got it completely wrong, that's just leftie propaganda.' I can remember Alex when he was underground press. Keen as mustard, looked just like Jim Morrison.

### 1979: round Dolly's house

Camilla, Dolly's young sister, 16. I hardly know her but this is one of those Maurice Chevalier moments when you realise growing up is beautiful. I ask her if she's ever been to the x club. Oh no, she shrieks, went there once, just horrible, rairly common. Dolly would never say that; just couldn't even think her grandparents' word.

### 1980: balls-up

'This is going to be a wonderful season for balls, the most glamorous, with people really dressed up

Echoes of Empire in 'The Jewel in the Crown': the Bombay Brasserie in Fulham Road

in the beautiful new taffetas. And it's all the old money, the real aristos this year, a return to real exclusivity – you have to admit they do it well' – girl gossip columnist sounding out copy on me.

### 1980: Dolly's again

Camilla, Dolly's sister, in off-the-shoulder taffeta. Just left school, no A-levels. What's she going to do? Well, she's the Girl of the Year, isn't she? 'Go to parties,' she says. She's in *Ritz* that month saying it. That dress was £500. Dolly was so low-profile at that age, she used to cut her surname in half so people wouldn't know (hated me calling her Dolly). But Camilla always uses the whole name and her title.

### 1981

'I hate her but she is . . . fascinating – oh come on Peter, admit it, she's got a lot of style' – former Labour candidate, now in fast publishing, on Mrs Thatcher.

### 1982: pre-Channel 4

'I expect it'll be all blacks and hideous lesbians – all that Ken Livingstone stuff. He needs shutting up' – the wing-collar boy. His habit costs £200 a week now.

### 1982: post-Falklands

'We've always been an Army family.' (First anyone's heard of it, sunshine.)

### 1983

'Oh, he's too delicious. He always wears white gloves' – journalist fan of John Carey.

### 1984

'I don't see why anyone should pay you anything, really' – right-wing thinker to complaining 18-year-old on YOPS scheme.

From about, say, 1975, Reactionary Chic has crept up on us like, oh, the world recession. It started with jokes, a little fun to raise the ante, a bit of liberal-baiting. (God, it was fun telling people to get their hair cut if you never cared for hippies – now, of course, they've done it and look what's happened.)

Over the last six or seven years there's been this box opened, and unbelievably, out have come the most incredible sentiments – now hold on – the most insensitive language, the most extraordinary symbols of . . . what? Forward into the past, backward into the future. Anyway, out have come basically all those things that no one would have given house-room to – not publicly anyway – in the early seventies because they were so horrid, or as a generation of liberals used to say, *reactionary*. There's a story that's been popping up in the world's alternative press ever since I've been reading it; the Gemstone theory. It's a conspiracy theory that claims to show Jack Kennedy was killed because of a 1930s plot involving Onassis and cartels and all that. Well, there's a story like that about *fashion* that I've heard often enough,

but I've never seen it written, namely that the CIA sought to encourage the military look as a Western fashion trend in the seventies as a counter to all the earlier anti-militarism – to make soldiers smart, etc. Actually I think my young friends got it wrong . . . at the time. But Army recruitment figures are up.

Let's get serious, let's talk about showing off. How could a person have made a stir among people of advanced taste – people who've been everywhere, man – in 1974. Sure as hell not with sex, drugs or rock and roll, nor with redistribution of money or saving whales, for these are basics of every little NW1 in the country (Manchester NW1, Leeds NW1). All the rebel imagery is used-up, banal.

Even the working classes are beginning to talk social-worker-speak in TV interviews. ('It's society's fault I done 'im in . . .')

So, sunshine, you cut your hair, get a tuxedo and say you believe in incentives and discipline. You can't go wrong. I mean, you'll make a stir. It'll

Anthony and Jeremy in this fall's strong menswear look: 'English-style' co-ordinates in 100 per cent wool-tweed effect. *Brideshead* was influential again from 1976

take till 1979 for the world to catch up. Everyone knows morality is part of the fashion trade now – it's design-led. People who lived for the look of the thing were recognising that straight-ahead modernism was just too drab, *because the battle was over*. There was no drama left, short of becoming Baader-Meinhof – which was a bit much for most parlour pinks.

When those Black Panthers crowded into Leonard Bernstein's drawing-room in 1970, what hit their audience about blacks' new role in American society? Their hairstyles. And, of course, some brilliantly calculated insults about white liberals. A positive workout.

The way the left got locked into a style rhetoric in the sixties and early seventies meant, of course, they could die by that particular sword, and it all started with fashion, with the dressing-up urge among grown-up liberals. It seemed harmless. Waiting in the wings, however, was a new generation who didn't have any ambivalent feelings; something aggressively stylish, radical-right and obviously unfair simply looked rather like forbidden fruit. The only two options for making a point, come the later seventies, were punk and Hard Gloss – the style of the new flaunt-it gossip columns. What they had in common was aggression and divisiveness: an instinct, one way or another, against the melting-pot, against the style of pluralism which by then was the everyday reality of Britain, not perfect, not disastrous, just there.

So it came to pass that the style-people came to Reactionary Chic about five years before recession tightened the belt and made it all *real*.

There were, of course, higher-brow, more verbal show-offs who took the reactionary mode as an opportunity. The tiny circle of Fleet Street/*Spectator* people described in Alan Watkins' *Brief Lives* all had a go when the high sixties was on its last legs, punch-drunk, unable to talk rationally or argue morally. Thus Peregrine Worsthorne in 1972, interviewing James Baldwin on television – an easy target for Oxbridge logic-chopping about the excesses of black politics – or Kingsley Amis bashing student power. The appeal of this sort of thing wasn't just the reassurance it gave the *Telegraph* reader; for a wider, less committed, group, it was a first taste of blood.

It just so happened, after the rhetoric of the high sixties, that all the intellectual energy – meaning the radical style – seemed to lie with the New Reactionaries, and they made the most of it. When they talked of unthinkable things like rules, discipline, logic and duty, voyeurs everywhere felt a *frisson* of delight. The silent majority geared up, and the left had forgotten how to respond, had lost its instincts. Auberon Waugh, you had to admit, was red-hot, the best underground comic around. Come the recession, the right was able to argue that redistribution of wealth should be put off for a better time. If we were forever redistributing, there would be nothing left. 'More means worse,' as Kingsley Amis had said about expanding higher education. We were ex-*growth*.

It was the end of guilt. Money Style, *le style Ritz*, looked attractive when there seemed to be less around. From the mid-seventies a Grand Hotel or country house was the backdrop for every other fashion shot. And, of course, period Rehab was the mood in housing and construction.

Mrs Thatcher had said 'rich men have rights too' and a new visible group of Young Fogeys seemed to be endorsing her and were written up frequently – and with much the same social implications – as, say, Richard Neville and Caroline Coon in the late sixties. They were the kind of sharp-end intelligentsia you'd do an interior spread on and ask for their observations on manners and know they'd ham it up and be *good copy*. Whether Mrs T. would really have gone a bomb on these fastidious young men with their twenties revival clothes and Gothic Revival homes is another question but Charles Moore and A. N. Wilson and all their little friends seemed to be endorsing a favourite Thatcher position, that *then* was better than *now* – and especially in Grantham.

By the later seventies, Reactionary Chic had become serious, no kidding; the guilt-free kids were flaunting it and saying it, the recession was well under way, and the first Thatcher government was in – not dilettante right-wing stylists,

HEY GOOD LOOKING

but the real thing. And the style Reactionary Chic aimed for by then had, for its fullest flowering, Old Resource, an imaginary upper-class style, the style of the people the pushy reactionary hustlers had replaced. God, how they liked it grand, the new hardnuts. Never had there been so much swirling of taffeta, so much planning of balls, such a cottage industry in gossip columns, such eagerness to get into what the columns still called ... stately homes.

This lurid Gainsborough video of a posh English past that built up in things like *Brideshead* (Waugh's love-affair with aristos, the hang-dog hopeless devotion the upper-middle class felt for grandees, filmed like decoration magazine spreads) or *Chariots of Fire* (filmed like a Hovis commercial, Euston Road admen go taffeta) suited the time perfectly, the *Easy Rider* and *Alice's Restaurant* of our day.

The new money, like the Edwardian money, wanted to dress up. The stylists wanted to dress up and so did the kids. And there was the new English-country-house style, the eighteenth century plus Winterhalter plus Edwardiana plus Wodehouse plus Waugh, all mixed up like a dream (the Lutyens/Raj revival). With 1981 – the Royal Wedding – and 1982 – the Falklands factor – we had, for the first time in ages (or more precisely, since the mid-sixties), a relevant international exportable look, flash and aggressive.

Abroad, the English aristocratic look had always had credibility, for who was better at rules and protocol and the lunatic gesture than the British? Years after anything newsworthy had happened, America started covering us again: our spectacular decay; our irresistible young Royalty (the three generations of the Royal Family always provoke American journalists to compare it with *Dallas* or *Dynasty*). Sinking beneath the waves in flaunt-it taffeta, with more video machines per head than anywhere in the world, we are a *story*.

In America the cycle has gone rather further. The silent majority found its voice sooner, and Ronnie and Nancy introduced Geriatric Fifties Suburban Reactionary Chic to Washington with a bang. All caddies and grey mink.

They claim – like Margaret Thatcher – that it's worked, the monetarism, the militarism, the tax-cut incentives. Capitalism has regained its robber-baron glamour and all the students want to work on Wall Street. If the banks don't crash, that is.

In Britain the change is mainly on the serious front: I mean in the style industry, which is bored with taffeta. Mrs Thatcher remains a peerless entertainer, spitting blood at archbishops: it took Alan Watkins to explain what should have been obvious all along; they like her for being nasty. Saatchi's make her have a big fight with somebody every six months. *Aggression* is her Reactionary Chic. Neil Kinnock does not know how to be offensive enough yet.

But the visuals have changed. The new mode – the new absurdity in the age of unemployment – is Work Style. Hard times for the enforced idle and the flaunt-it kids. There is a tide of little symbols (obscene frivolity you may say, but these things speak volumes): Robert Elms' recent tongue-in-cheek 'Hard Times' article in *The Face*; the pioneer look in fashion photography; Katherine Hamnett's lugubrious legible clothing with bomb-banning messages; the denim revival; the way Fleet Street briefly turned on the Princess of Wales.

At the New Year round-up, a telly journalist called me for an 'in' and 'out' list. What about fashion, she says. Ask the fashion girls, I say. I give her some names, She's back an hour later, bemused. The girls have all said it's thumbs down to taffeta and all that. It's something leaner, quieter altogether, more Left Bank. Next year, they're using the docks a lot for background. And sixties-look offices. Think Quant revival, I tell her. Anything for a laugh.

W·O·R·L·D·S

A·P·A·R·T

### A night on the tiles

Emergency Ward 10. And the trolley goes down the New Brutalist concrete ramp into the basement, round the corner and into . . . a laboratory? a main service area? a gym? a men's room? Anyway, past reception it's all white tiled, every living inch of it's white tiled, with those not-quite glossy white tiles with the special grouting you get in shops with the Italian Look. There's no Italian Look here, though, in fact there's no look at all here except the white-tiled look, because there's nothing here. I mean, no exhibits. Where are the exhibits, the hand tools used by authentic craftsmen promised in the invitation? Where's the hammer with the terrific ergonomic surfaces shaped by the synergy of a 1910 ten-shilling-a-week man and his tool, where's the plane with the hand-carved decoration, plucked from the life for the collecting wall of a man with a knit tie just off Primrose Hill, with a Victorian fairground horse in the window bay?

It takes a while to suss out where the *exhibits*, so to speak, actually are in the Victoria and Albert Museum's Boilerhouse annexe exhibition of hard tools. There is, however, one irresistible tableau in the Hyper-Realist style, the best thing there. On the far right hand there *seems* to be a kind of window with venetians against it, and if you peer in there seems to be *a young man with everything* on display in an office interior in the style popularly known as Hi-Tech. And this young man *seems* to wear a bow-tie, a perky but tasteful daytime bow-tie of the kind worn on special occasions by those who have been to art school, and everything else a modern person should have.

It must be something like those American sculptures of elderly tourists with every sag, every class-correct detail of polyester outwear rendered amazingly in modern materials. And it's there to make the point about Art Businesses, or something like that. When it moves, however, one realises it's little Stephen Bayley, who runs the show here, living the Design Life.

### Chic graphique

Frank couldn't be more graphic if he wore the Habitat check fabric and a rule in his shirt-pocket. Frank had the Ruthless Roman, the early sixties Italian Look jazz modern crop when his hair went, so now that's graphic too, cross-hatched on his scalp in very low relief. He has the wrap-around facial trim instead, very neatly cut back, and all the other little signs that the Freemasonry of the square make to each other, like significant specs – interesting opticals are a big thing round here – with big lenses framed in a nice raspberry jelly material. He also has his shirt – dark greyish-blue denim – buttoned up with no tie. No tie! Only someone with a real Design Centre Index memory would think to do that number. (Frank *has* a tie for this shirt, in pale pink knitted silk with a blunt end, very like the kind he first wore as a mid-teenager in the Beatle boom, only much better quality.)

And excellent charcoal flannels – that really thick, soft shiny flannel the Milanese millionaires have their suits in. Besides the tie, Frank has always, but always, loved *good* grey flannel, and he's always loved girls who are slightly bandy like Julie Christie – and from about the same time. Ditto the loafers, which are actually Bass Weejuns in the classic colour bought in that shop in Covent Garden that specialises in the Ivy style, just like the place in Richmond he went to in the sixties. Plus the Argyll socks with the pink and grey patterns. These classic American designs just are *perfect*, like their diners and Mack trucks. The plain hard pale metal, camera-case colour. Frank uses a silvery camera-case for his stuff – and for the big layouts he's got this amazing corrugated see-through plastic thing, ten times lighter and sharper than an art bag.

Graphic Frank's beardless brother Harry checks out the action in Paul Smith's: Harry carries brushed-aluminium camera case, striped cotton preppy jacket, artistic bowtie, big red specs, navy-blue textile Oxfords with light soles. Solid Fabian-fellwalker footwear awaits

Frank's just won his second *D and A D* award, for a series of books on the new cookery, Minceur, Nouvelle, etc., all based on a square-printed background with kind of squared-up food on it done with a computer graphics effect (mocked-up actually). Frank did the covers, and when they make it for Channel 4 next year he's going to do the titles. TV titles are a big thing now, the designers get their credits on-screen. Maybe he'll get a BAFTA. Strictly speaking, though, he's a packaging man. Edwardian lady typefaces for wholewheat biscuits, fine red overchecks on white for a new aftershave, that kind of thing. Mainstream but good. Classic really.

While Frank's mainstream – it's quite a big practice now and he really does more managing than actual layouts and, more and more, when he's presenting to clients he's wearing the Paul Smith suits which look straight as anything but have some really nifty touches – he's still pretty eclectic. He's not like the guys in their forties and fifties who were brought up on the frozen Swiss International look and *Graphis* annual and all that, and never recovered. He often jokes about the Polish cartoon look. Frank knows what it is to slope along Wardour Street with a new Atlantic single on import ready for the old Dansette (actually he'd never have had anything as naff as a Dansette in 1966, but it's a reference – a bit of roots – he finds increasingly relevant now that some of his juniors – 22 and fresh out of the LCP – are crazy about all that period).

## The rise of the gridniks

Designer taste, the taste of the graphics, now controls the aesthetic of really large organisations of every kind, from multiple retailers to government departments. Designer taste dominates middle-class print media – and especially magazines. The look of almost everything you buy, read, or watch, reflects not so much the world it was made in, but Design Land. Ten to one the makers will have got in someone from Covent Garden, perhaps the people who did those new yoghurts to look like eggcups, or the man who did the *Büro Landschaft* in the new Esso building. Designer taste rubs off on just about everyone above the social Plimsoll mark. Ever thought about a rubber floor? Nylon door pulls? A white-tiled tabletop?

You don't avoid Conranism by not going to Habitat. Conran's own design practice works for all the big businesses, and there are half a dozen other design practices which are as big as – and commercially more important than – the larger advertising agencies. Covent Garden rules Bradford and Bristol. Anywhere big business is uncertain, or downhearted, it now looks to a shot of design magic – disciplined and basic, yet creative at the same time – to revitalise its business, its shopping centre. Good design sells, they said in the sixties and now, in the eighties, industrialists believe it. After all Design Land speaks their language, the language of big government, of business, of profit per square foot selling space. Design businesses talk, well, MBA talk now.

The essentials laid bare: beams, pipes and at the far end a rain hopper. The monochrome viewer misses the primary red couture taps and reinforcement on the beams. Note also classic Mies van der Rohe chairs, custom-built counter-top and original 1930s chromium-covered coffee-pot

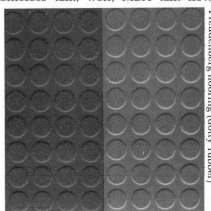

Freudenberg flooring (dotty rubber)

There's none of this wouldn't-it-be-nice-ism or stuff about heavenly green swags. It's a man's world in design.

What they're putting over, one way and another, is a version of the world-view of, say, a couple of hundred people in the West End and NW1 in 1966, the taste of the sixties media and commercial/visual classes which has evolved to become the taste of what Americans call Yuppies – Young Urban Professionals – *absolutely everywhere* in the eighties. Mainstream designer taste, at the less exotic levels, expresses, after all, what matters to a modern manager – it's systematic, flexible, interchangeable, logical. It observes constraints. It's mobile, it updates. You can sketch out the scheme *and* how to administer it. And the decoration side's pretty undemanding.

But it's fun too. You can change everything – the offices, the letterheads, the product packs – knowing it's quite safe in the hands of these men who go into the company archives for the sepia photographs of the chairman's grandfather, and talk like systems analysts.

Thus does it all truly come not just from the Bauhaus to our house, but from Covent Garden, Islington, King's Road 1974, Beaubourg and New York lofts, to their shops, your beer can, his offices and the Ministry's advertising.

In the sixties advertising was the key glamour trade and there was a cottage industry in *worry books* following the 'hidden persuaders' line that it was massively powerful and possibly dangerous – affected all our lives; distorted our view of the real world; was politically dangerous – that sort of thing. But Design Land is dealing in *real things*. The office stays fixed up the following day, the shops go on looking different. It's the solid state of persuasion.

Of course advertising itself is full of design types and the graphic taste is the ruling mode in the advertising homes Out West, in Fulham and Richmond, Barnes and Sheen. But the design types don't *need* advertising now, they're a class of their own. Now a designer is a recognised type of person.

Behind it all is a world of men and women

### The graphic wardrobe

The graphic wardrobe is *organised* on the eternal principles: simplicity, 'modern classic' design, obvious functionalism, etc. (if they could *wear* a van der Rohe they would). And they look amazingly clean. But *younger* Graphics want to be groovy too, not uptight, and this means problems. They're taught to despise the obviously poppy/fashiony and they can't relate to Jermyn Street except in small doses. So the main looks are still engineers-of-the-modern-world or, for the younger ones, various versions of cartoon 'America' from about 1953. They prefer a Look from a Book. Graphics are the biggest object fetishists going. They get completely fixated on *the* design object, so perfect, classic, etc.

- Levis 501s are one thing they can share with more clubbable groovers, because they're archaic, classical, functional, work clothes.
- Very obviously real, brown leather shoes in heavy archaic patterns – Fabian fell-walkers – are particularly favoured by serious-

thinking Graphics, especially architectural ones, who've read a lot of illustrated biographies.
- Brown Oxfords.
- Bass Weeguns (classic Americana).
- Kickers (for the foreignness, exposed stitching, etc, rather than the babyness).
- Brooks Boots, the broad white punched American sportswear boots (one in three advertising agency art-department men wears Brooks).
- Fairisle pullovers over white collarless shirts.
- Bow-ties: Graphics wear bow-ties at every opportunity *except* for formal occasions when they are mandatory – when they protest with open and collarless shirts. They favour the obviously clip-on narrow fifties American ones.
- Knitted wool ties – especially in horizontal stripes – are key. Old Graphics had them in the early sixties, when they were a big

design thing and younger ones wear them as their lip service to New Wave.
- Socks: Graphics can be very creative with socks – pastel socks and loafers and the rediscovered Argyll in pale yellow- or pink-based patterns are particularly graphic. The ankle's the erogenous zone.
- They like pastel sweater and socks combos from S. Fisher.
- Artistic knitwear as a whole is pretty big in Graphicland. It doesn't seem quite so poppy as other colourful stuff because it's a Work of Art.
- Above all, Graphics love Paul Smith. Paul Smith is *the* Graphic's Own Designer. He understands how to break a fashion to them gently, he understands these important Euro-influences (the Milan Designer look), he knows the materials and colours they like, and sells all their totem objects – the pens, watches,

Top Shop,
'Star Wars'
pop graphique
by Fitch

educated on graph paper to think in squares, of proper designing by numbers. The world of the design solution – modular, conceptual, systematic – to life's problems like corporate identity, shelf impact, or page traffic (meaning keeping them looking).

There's almost nothing you can't find a design solution to. The whole of Design Land's climbed so far, so fast, and all of it really post-war. It's got an amazingly consistent view when you really get down to it, has designer world. Before the war, and really up until the late fifties, designers weren't usually trained as designers – they didn't actually *do* graphics – they just learnt a trade. Designing the Covent Garden way didn't really happen much before the war. With books, for instance, you were either an artist 'doing' a book, or the printer's layout man. Chairs in tortured metal were designed by architects with Bauhausey names like van der Rohe, chairs in elm and ash were made by Morrisey artist/craftsmen called something like Gordon Russell. *Commercial art*

The younger graphic hankers after the Hiram Holliday look and touch of the practical stylings

photography books, etc, they go for. Last Christmas *every* Graphic got the scarlet Paul Smith cashmere scarf.
- Graphic trad: recently some made-it Graphics have gone for a colouring-book version of Jermyn Street suitable for period sets and suchlike. They like Turnbull and Asser shirts, knitted alpaca waistcoats and other studio properties.

**Graphic grooming**

The graphic innovation is the *wrap-around* – the short, even-length, all-over beard/moustache kit, particularly favoured by older Graphics who have lost their hair. This look derives from late fifties jazzbeards and the Milan Designer look.

Graphic haircuts tend to be short and functional. The graphic reaction – delayed – to punk was the *clipped* look, short hair under control like a lawn: Graphics in advertising – the less purist ones have sometimes gone for the Video

Fruzzle, a subtler version of Martin Shaw's footballer curls. But the Ruthless Roman, short, brushed forward late fifties modern, still rules.

Graphics don't aim to look too sexy.

**Graphic accessories**

Graphics come into their own with accessories; they wear odd things *no one* else wears. Small objects, perfectly designed, thrill them more than precious metals – they avoid precious metals, it's against the training. Graphics go for special specs, especially from Cutler and Gross. (Tony Gross is a major figure in graphic circles.)
- Primary coloured ones -- red, blue and graphic green. Models – Patrick Hughes, Hockney, etc.
- Special sunspecs – out-takes from their favourite old movies – particularly Ray-Bans.

was what Quentin Crisp used to do when he painted plaster pigs for butchers' shops. They hadn't invented design consultants then.

After the war, though, it all got pulled together into *design* – given a great send off by twinkling, donnish, pipe-smoking gents like Paul (now Lord) Reilly at the Festival of Britain. The ultra planning mode of the big architect and the big designers was starting.

They had to be educated though. Consumer Land in America, the shiny world of rationing – free, coated paper magazines and FMCG – fast moving consumer goods like detergents and chocolate and face cream – was the example. Media and two-dimensional design was an integrated discipline. And three-dimensional commercial designers like Norman Bel Geddes and Raymond Leowy were already publicised *stars* with big businesses consulting to big corporations.

## Square roots

As the gridniks came out and rose irresistibly to greatness on the back of simplicity and efficiency – anything but styling – so the grid itself took over. By the later seventies, wherever you looked their triumphal decorative motif appeared on everything ... *squares*. What symbolised our time more than the wholesale application of the graphicals' little working pattern motif, the little maths book, cash book – 35p at Smith's – as an ornament? From the mid-seventies on, the grid appeared *on* things as a decorative flourish in its own right. If the modern movement had ruthlessly stripped the layers of Edwardian Adam plasterwork, rococo revival, Deco reliefs, and fifties chrome shams (let's be honest, that car *can't* fly ...), then in the seventies the designers stamped squares on anything they could see. Screw honesty to function, tonight is what it means to be semi-young.

The mark of the beast went on everything. There was the *white tile mania*, where tile moved out of the sanitary areas and armour-plated floors and walls everywhere; *mesh madness*, where squared steel mesh – so systematic, so Hi-Tech – became the dominant theme of a thousand shop refits. And of course there was *wired glass*, the solid state

---

Pens – Graphics are naturally mad on the instruments of their trade – pens in particular. High fetish objects are:
- The Mont Blanc, the cigar-sized, fat black with all the overstated virtues of the schoolboy Osmiroid.
- Lamy everything. Lamy is very designery and Milany and Hi-Tech. Matt black, flexy rubber bits and a black nib all make this *the* pen.
- Old Watermans in marbled Bakelite.
- Period Americana ball-points with stripping blondes, etc, down the side.

- Matt black action watches from Paul Smith.
- Filofax or Creative Handbook Diary systems.
- American yellow writing-pads.

- Dunhill lighters with the little armature.
- Zippo lighters.
- Gitanes, Camels, Marlboros: all 'design statement' packs – English cigarettes are avoided.
- High design, adjustable lamps, like the big Anglepoise type from Gaetano Pesco and the Tizio lamps.

Cases: no Graphic has an ordinary briefcase when there's a more interesting design solution like:
- Camera-cases in silvery metal
- The fishing bag in leather-trimmed beige canvas, with mesh pockets on the outside
- The one-piece moulded polythene case in designer primaries – *that* green, yellow, blue, etc.
- A battered brown old Orient Express case
- A *clear plastic* case – see at a glance
- A metal mesh case for easy ventilation and the Hi-Tech look, sprayed a nice designer primary

**The graphic home**

English Graphics find it difficult to be as purist as their severe European counterparts. They go for high design statements and Hi-Tech but get distracted by whimsy and pop fashions and so they lose the thread. Besides, all that Euro stuff is *very* expensive.

Habitat *is* basic graphic taste – no serious Graphic acknowledges it now but all the squarey tile stuff and the feel for primary colours and authenticity show the sixties graphic eye. And Habitat, after all, had *the check fabric called 'Graph'*.

Graphics live in Islington, Primrose Hill, Notting Hill Gate, Wapping, Shoreditch.

The graphic home has been endlessly rethought and redone. But not *decoration*. They don't go in for decoration in that sense.

The house will aim for a cool *design statement* – space not clutter – graphic colours – currently primaries and neon pastels against grey and black, and lots of tiles.

of mesh, mesh in aspic, lifted from the purely burglar-proof to the coffee-table class, surrounded by bolt-on, component, Kwik-cast alloy legs of what appeared to be piping made for industrial buildings.

And the propaganda for the square! Did Goebbels make every book and magazine in the Reich bear the swastika on every page? You couldn't move for squares: wherever a middle-market magazine art-director wanted something looking a bit Covent Gardeny, systematic or faintly digital, on went the squared overlays. And on the most unlikely things. Squares became the background to every kind of exotic, sinuous, real life disorderly thing you could draw or photograph, giving the effect that somehow they were either on laboratory dissecting tables or – more likely – not there at all, just computer simulations sent down the line.

Advertisers too favoured the grid look to show computer age, challenge-of-the-eighties people and situations, and used it to sell home electronics and objects which *wished* to be electronic – cars

for instance. The newest wrinkle in graphical advertising, where design grid met systems and the grid glowed green and came alive in three dimensions, was something called computer graphics. With computer graphics you could sort of draw things in electronic space on a TV screen and move them about till they were perfect and then a computer-controlled machine tool would zap them out. This magic process fed back into advertising where the design and systems of bog standard fleet cars for reps were displayed as a set of glowing, green, three-dimensional grids. The car was a micro-system, a holograph, anything but a lump of 1895 Birmingham-made pressings and castings. Disco grids. Sometimes all this gridding gave a very surreal effect, square upon square, as of a perspective trick, where everything was truly flat – all graphic art aspires to the condition of flatness – and would soon vanish back into a book.

Today's Designer Land evolved during the late sixties and early seventies as a kind of branch of business consultancy. Design's great breakthrough came in the merger fever of the sixties,

One particular bright green is *the* graphic colour – they use it everywhere, work, home, everything. And particularly in the nylon graphic door handles and other fittings you find wherever basic graphic is spoken.

Graphics prefer *flat* pictures – illustrations, designs, etc – graphics in fact. They favour the kind of artist represented by Francis Kyle or the Thumb Gallery: Adrian George – much used by graphic art directors because of the pastel Hockneyishness – Glyn Boyd Harte – graphic jokes on a checkered tablecloth. These are often framed in a Minimalist way with plain glass and clips. Graphics also believe in Photography as an Art Form. They *buy* photographs in signed editions and put them up like pictures.

The bathroom and kitchen will have had a lot of attention. There will be yards of plain white tiles – the small *industrial* rectangular white tile is particularly graphical. It covers floors, walls, and other surfaces – everything but the ceiling.

Certain Hi-Tech tokens are totally graphic – a clear glass cylinder for flowers, laboratory beakers for glasses, aluminium buckets as the table centrepiece. (And *tulips*, because they make a composition very like an *illustration*.)

What's black and white and red all over? The Gridnik Astrohome, with exclusive waste-graph-paper-basket and baby-grid pencil-holders

True Graphics almost always have plain white china – albeit with a little coloured line on it (and usually the kind that stacks). They go for those big white chamfered café française type cups all advertising agencies have. It goes perfectly with a Chemex, a cafetière, or any other foreign movie type coffee device.

Graphics took all that Hi-Tech stuff to heart so they'll always have the difficult-to-get catering range instead of the happy domestic one in avocado enamel. They'll also search out the special Euro designer handles and taps in primary plastics – the ones the local builder's merchant doesn't have.

Other little giveaways come in the treatment of functional stuff like pipes, old radiators, bare brick constructional details. Graphics don't believe in putting these in a pretty box as in Belgravia

when the collective vanity of British business was to look big through acquisition and the application of a bit of American-style corporate cosmetics. Corporate cosmetics was actually something called corporate identity and in America it was done by design houses. When Anthony Wedgwood Benn – as they called him then – and the IRS prodded dinosaurs to mate, designers found themselves called into mahogany boardrooms to do their stuff.

This business of designing the corporate identity was all rather abstract and high-flown. When knighted artists who knew the chairman's wife had done out the head-office hall in 1935, or when 'shop fitters' – as they called them then – had fixed up the shop in Birmingham, there'd been none of this. But these sixties designers were completely different. They'd ask you what your company really did, what its philosophy was and how people related to it, and ask to see the company archives and talk to the senior management. And they sent memos about it all. You'd think they were management consultants from the way they

carried on, not sign-painters. Then, months later, there'd be a presentation with slides in a darkened boardroom where they'd show you an embarrassing collection of your buildings or vans, your letterheads or packs, all different or gauche and cheesy and usually old-fashioned too. And there'd be the horror stories, where they'd have found what the local management had done to the shop interior or the windows, and you'd really cringe.

Then came the solution, the design solution, the answer to all the grim, cheesy, disorganised, 1947 reality of the mega corps' interface with its publics – for the mega corp had many publics to be upset by a sign; horrified by a letterhead; sickened by a shop window. And out would come ... *a logo*, some kind of little wiggly graphic version of the corporation initials – say, NHS combined into a curious little sign like a child's international symbol for a thatched cottage, or a three-legged affair like the Isle of Man thing. And some type, *typography*, modern honed-down Penguin Special type reflecting the modernity, internationality and diversity of your business.

or Ilford, nor even painting them to match, they *make a feature* of them – old radiators in primaries – copper pipes actually *polished*, and so forth.

Graphics have an exaggerated respect for *tools* of any kind – design tools especially, kitchen tools, etc. – and turn them into tableaux, collections, at the drop of a hat. The moment you see splendid pens and sharp pencils fanned out in a commemorative mug, or wooden spoons in one of those old beige and brown jars, or teaspoons in an old Keiller marmalade pot, you know you're in mid-period graphic. Graphics also collect brands for their *packaging* – all those mustards, teas, coffees and funny Third World brands mounted as Art.

Graphics' dream homes aren't *houses* at all: they're warehouses, lofts – *acres of space* – converted Shoreditch factories, pumping stations. A consortium of Graphics will probably buy Battersea power station to convert into homes of character, keeping as much of the machinery as they can.

They like minimal furniture with lots

of emphasis on leather. Very rarely anything pre-1880. Favoured Victorian tends towards the jokey or 'industrial':
- Early wooden filing cabinets.
- 'Patent' devices, *not* domestic High Victorian.
- 'Deco' is still basically OK.

Gridnik heaven, Astrohome, Neal Street, Covent Garden, 1984

The graphic dream furniture is still van der Rohe, Corbusier – and Eileen Gray for the more knowledgeable. They still want a Barcelona or a Grand Comfort.

The Bertoia stretched-grid chair is an excellent token in the meanwhile, and almost affordable. (Sotheby's and Christie's 'modern classics' sales are attractive but often unaffordable.) The mainstream dream shop is Scott Howard in Berners Street and Aram Designs, Artemede/Takis and sometimes Hille are still on the list. Real life involves more Habitat than they like to admit. Younger Graphicals go for the easy fifties pastiche of Tommy Roberts' Practical Styling (cut-price Memphis) or One Off.

### How to set a graphical table

The ideal graphical table is very flat. Graphics do not go in for the cliffs of silver candlesticks, topiary and flowers flavoured by other types.

The ideal is the army kit-inspection principle – all items of the same dimen-

They'd explain how the logo – the sign – represented some essential part of what you did – a solution based on a wheel shape for the transport conglomerate, or how a half opened V with some stripes inside it meant printing and publishing, and so on.

The clients were spellbound, especially if they were New Men. The awful heritage of sixty years of the founder and his senile homilies about pile it high and sell it cheap or make a better mousetrap, was wiped away in this sophisticated, civilised simplicity; it was the only way.

Then they showed you the book – the manual. The manual explained exactly how the three-legged thing and the three rows of type were to be applied to everything – the sizes, typefaces, colours and finishes that were mandatory for every activity to show the face of the corporation – modern, flexible, technological, civilised, etc. – in every one of its activities. Arthur Camshaft Pressings (Blackburn), acquired 1948, would give up its wally script and its line about 'suppliers of quality pressings at competitive prices since 1885' and the proud line-drawing of the New Works (1938). It became Arthur Camshaft: the pressings division of XYZ. Since a lot of very different businesses were seeking something of the kind in the sixties – something modern, corporate, international and so forth – a lot of them came out redesigned to the hilt, face-lifted to die.

Twelve years later they'd be having in new design teams who went down the archives again and fished up the sepia photographs of the founder and Albert Camshaft and the demi-Modernist exterior of the New Works with little squeals of pleasure. Lads with primary green briefcases made of washing-up bowl plastic would explain that their current logo and namestyle was a sixties horror, while customers could relate to the Albert Camshaft identity. Hereafter all the pressings' packaging should feature Albert and his first foreman in a sort of oval barbershop vignette on sepia-coloured paper.

God, the relief for the Young Turks after twelve years of this business acting like it's the bloody Civil Service or something, with the world owing

sions aligned by a piece of string used as a horizontal plumb-line. A planking type surface is fine (one-way lines) but grid-reinforced glass is perfect. On it you have chopsticks or ex-NAAFI type knives and forks, very flat white plates, clear plastic pepper and (sea)salt, and all the silver and white tones. The glasses will be plain, heavy, or labora-

Off-the-peg graphique with
Moderne Art overtones

tory, unless they're fun plastic from Astrohome.

### Graphics' food and drink

Graphics aren't really foodies: they're more interested in the presentation; colour theming, landscaping on the plate (the *look* of Cuisine Minceur with all those *flat* colourful bits on white plates appeals enormously.) Thus Graphics will give you an all-red meal or an all-white one. They eat out a lot and their eating is very fashion orientated. What they like is simple, light, modern. Thematic and difficult to get – food that shows you've been around.

Every kind of interesting-looking delicatessen and import thing has been graphic in its time. Taramasalata during the pink period, every variety of olive. Japanese food is graphic heaven, the Tokyo/LA connection is very big with slightly younger Graphics. 'Good' food, however, is what you get in restaurants, and Graphics go to restaurants run by people who understand them, like L'Escargot. Graphic drink, equally, is chosen for its bottle graphics or its references. Graphics were early in on Perrier, and American beer with its archaic labels (Becks, Budweiser). Through Zanzibar they were very early in on the cocktail revival too. So much kitschy colour to look at. You won't find your average Graphic with his head in a cellar book though.

### Graphic heights and heroes

Graphics admire:

- Anything Bauhaus – including the graphics, more than ever now!
- Milan
- The Pompidou Centre
- The Lloyds building in the City
- Japanese gardens
- The Museum of Modern Art
- New York generally
- The Eiffel Tower
- Kings Cross Station
- La Maison Verre in Paris
- Victorian steel-framed buildings, especially industrial
- They feel *odd* about Conran, Habitat and the V & A Boilerhouse

it a living! And clever old Nigel – graduate intake 1954 – with all his Ecology Party drivel about social responsibility and corporate priorities and his safari jackets – had been responsible for the sixties do-over, typical waffle merchant stuff; straight out of those old Harvard Business School case-studies he loved quoting.

But really, Design Land is historical, or rather history is cut-outs to graphics. The history they're interested in is the history of commercial art, of industrial design. Two-dimensional pioneers of advertising, Victorian commercial typefaces. History's just something else on the paste-up; you lift it out, blow it up, borrow it for an effect like classical statuary – against the grid, of course.

The graphic education is remarkably self-contained, modern. It's a couple of illuminated manuscripts then quickly on to 1890, the books you have to read, and thence to Bauhaus. The books you have to read aren't too theoretical; design doesn't have its critique, its church of scholars or even yet its party political factions yet – it's apolitical, businesslike. That's to come.

Heroes are:
- Milton Glazer (Push Pin Studios) who made graphic so big
- 'Ferry' Porsche
- Gropius
- Charles Eames
- Early Americana like the Golden LA people – Jan and Dean and the Beach Boys
- The Everly Brothers
- Cary Grant (what style!)
- The Duke of Windsor (ditto)
- Norman Parkinson (ditto)
- Bruce Weber (a Paul Smith act)
- American fifties comic strip artists
- Cavalcante (GP film unit thirties production)

Can a *woman* be a Graphic? This interesting subject has been debated for years, like the question of women as, say, pilots. The graphic sensibility is definitely lads' stuff at heart, although women can adopt it, work with it, proselytise for it, and all that. Women on magazines or in PR, for instance, marry Graphics, and fix up a nice graphic house. But sometimes, in the

• Can girls be Graphique?

middle of all these white tiles, you think you see a flash of some impure yearnings for the . . .

**Graphic horrors**

Graphics feel deeply about the unenlightened reactionary clutter represented by:
- *Architectural Digest*
- *Interiors*
- Herbaceous borders
- Laura Ashley
- Harrods' furnishing and kitchens
- Stockbroker Tudor
- Jaguar saloons

Instead there are magazines. Designers live in and through magazines, on the colour-printed page. History is fifties collectors' issues of *Look* and *Harpers Bazaar*. The play of Ideas comes through *Zoom* and *The Face* (they're taking *The Face* now, even Frank's generation). Designers are magazine freaks and a half.

**Golden days**

Designer Land is coming of age. Never have designer types had so much to spend in Zanzibar, their very own club. And – arise Sir Terence – Conran is a knight, a captain of industry. The Boilerhouse is a national show place for designerism, Conran-supported. Will he endow a chair of design at Cambridge next? The Conran Foundation: it sounds like the Ford Foundation or the Getty Museum. It's all big stuff.

And, at last, somewhere a place for us, there's the new Covent Garden, opened in 1980 and already a world centre of the graphic perspective on life. Covent Garden is Design World, England's first taste of what a fully planned environment

- Geoffrey Bonsack
- The Savoy Grill

and most other examples of the conventional plutocratic sex-and-money-on-toast look. They know 'good' taste is less definable now, but they still find it hard going.

**Graphic cars**

Citroën remains *the* graphic car image, from the early police car to the 2CV to the pneumatic Pallas. They also like Fiats because they're so design-y in their colours and detailing, and the soft-top VWs because they're so classic and functional. Younger Graphics into Americana may be Kustom Kar boys, with a Chevy or so out front – you can have fun on the King's Road and hire them out for your friends' commercials. Actually, most Graphics drive 2CVs, Renault 5TLs, Volkswagen Golf GTI convertibles, etc, and some older ones have mellowed through the ad agency ranks into the BMWs, and the flash made-it Graphic gone pop-star wants a *proper* Porsche 928.

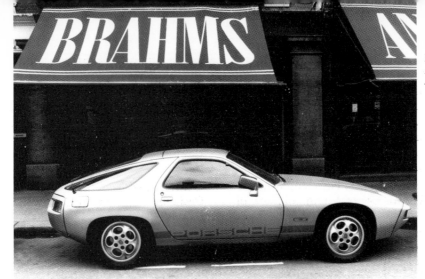

Made it!
A 928!!!
– *and* getting Liszt

could feel like – because there's nothing, literally nothing, in Covent Garden which hasn't been thought out by the square men, there's no corner undesigned. *Everyone* in Covent Garden speaks Graphic. Every graphic obsession is represented, from the giant NW1 Rehab of the market building itself to the green and white designers' offices, to the piazza space where middle-class street entertainers introduce their acts in that Late Hippie Victorian artisan tone they all effect – you can *see* their announcements set in the jolly Victorian Commercial type graphics love, with little pointing fingers – *before your very eyes; in front of the crowned heads of Europe.*

### Graphic venues

Zanzibar in Covent Garden is *the* graphic venue for ad men, designers, illustrators – all the high-income visual service businesses. Also:

- Chelsea Arts Club
- Architectural Association bar – very much the grey look
- The Neal Street Restaurant
- Joe Allen's (American theme park)

Demi-graphic girls in search of Ugandan liaisons with artistic Golf owners. Reply Box No 69, *Campaign*

- L'Escargot – ice-cream *eau-de-Nil* stage set
- 192 Kensington Park Road (spot the designer allusions)
- Café Pacifico
- The Caprice (very sixties pastiche)
- Any Japanese restaurant
- Soho Brasserie – so convenient for video land – the new frontier
- Most Covent Garden wine bars

### Graphic institutions and events

The Hilton never took so much money as when they started doing *the D and AD awards*. All those scruffy-looking jerks they'd worried about *spent* to high heaven – the liqueurs went along the tables like a conveyor belt. Those boys can spend – and drink. Particularly the advertising agency Graphics.

The *dip shows* at most major art schools – Kingston, Hornsey (Middlesex polytechnic) and the RCA degree show. It's interesting to see what the kids are doing now:

- Designers' 'open house' drinks parties on summer Saturdays

- Advertising agency parties
- Private views at graphically-oriented galleries like Francis Kyle, Thumb and Graffiti or the Photographers Gallery
- Graphic garden parties in the Richmond area

### Graphic jobs

Graphic has spread far just beyond design – it's the ruling aesthetic in all these design-conscious service businesses sown so thickly in Covent Garden and Soho. The 'creative' – and many other – parts of advertising agencies are graphical; all 'design houses', it goes without saying; many PRs, commercials and video production companies; magazine and trade paperback publishers; parts of the record business (though they can get very impure). Architects, who got a lot of it started, have got rather overshadowed, though many have the same tastes.

Sir Terence has plans
for his newest acquisition –
Heal's of Tottenham Court Road

## D·E·S·I·G·N·T·I·M·E

# N·W·1'S
# F·I·R·S·T
# F·A·M·I·L·Y

How much more impactful the Conrans are, in retrospect, than those other sixties people, how much more mainstream, how much ... bigger. I mean, Terence's Habitat holding alone was valued at at least £25 million during the flotation in 1980 and that was before he started to take over the whole High Street (Mothercare in the spring of 1982, then Richard Shops in 1983). Shirley's first novel, *Lace,* had a million-dollar American advance from Simon & Schuster, which was the biggest ever for a first novel, and that was before the Lorimar miniseries, the merchandise, all the add-tos. And the boys, you have to admit, are remarkable. Everyone knows Jasper and Sebastian.

The Conrans are NW1's own form of royalty: the sixties Visuals who took over the world, stayed the course and penetrated into the heart of it. Can you think of another name that says so many of the right things? No wonder they all use it. It has all the definitive marks of alternative royalty. The husband and former wife are famous; it works across two generations; it means more than just money: it means a certain style of life. The Conran Story would make a good paperback. They catch the imagination: the first art-school dynasty, those Conrans of Regent's Park.

When the first Habitat opened in 1964, Terence Conran was fond, as who was not then, of comparing his business to Mary Quant's. It was *design-led*, part of the excitement. By the eighties – and especially at the time of the Habitat stock-market flotation – he tended to talk about Marks & Spencer and Sainsbury's, and cite Habitat's use of computer tills. (And it wasn't 'trendy' – how he disliked that word. Trendy was no longer where it was at.)

Habitat was the solid state, the perfect expression, of a whole class of person that had hardly existed before the sixties. (London NW1 was only the smartest, richest end of it.) Such a coincidence of aspiration and consumption and unanswerable

Shirley Conran can cope with anything

rightness; the kind of person who read the *Ob-server* and, later, the women's pages of the *Daily Mail*. Knock through the rooms of the 1880s terrace cottage ('Let the sunshine in'), on with the brilliant white, sand and seal the boards, up with the bookshelves. Can you think of a universal look today that's anything like it? (Rag rolling, festoons, faux marbling – don't make me laugh.)

Conran didn't invent the look but he synthesised it, proselytised for it, and made it accessible. He added the right grace-notes with the chicken bricks and the other basic, simple *batterie*

*de cuisine* type things you could read about in the Penguin Elizabeth David. You may laugh. But 'Life and Times in NW1', the Alan Bennett and Marc comic-strip television series, was fifteen years ago, more. The satirical potential has worn thin. (It's no coincidence that Posy Simmonds's 'Mrs Weber's Diary' is in the *Guardian*, whose readers still have such houses.)

The *scale* of Habitatisation is undeniable. It was a new career in a new room. A career in the new service of the State perhaps, a plate-glass university or a social-work department, planning or architecture. Or as one of the new graduate kind of businessman, in marketing or corporate planning, in fast-moving consumer goods. Despite the apparent differences, they shared a world-view.

These kinds of people, liberated by education in the late sixties and early seventies, moved into the convergent mainstream from different backgrounds. First-generation graduates – respectable working and lower-middle class – joined the children of the more established middle and upper-middle class, all recruited into Habitat classlessness. The transit lounge to the New World. Habitat expressed the way thousands of people with ostensibly different backgrounds wanted to see the future. They shared the aesthetic of the Simple.

conventional public-school types; Bryanston makes arty-crafty boys, not Army officers and City Solids, and Paulinas are bluestockings rather than Young Ladies. (Shirley's classmates, her immediate competitors, were two other Shirleys, Williams and Summerskill.) And they both went on to art school. Shirley to Portsmouth, where she sometimes wore Balenciaga and rather stood out, and Terence to the Central in London, where he did textiles. Thus far, there is a certain similarity with their friends and contemporaries, the Plunket-Greenes (Alexander was at Bryanston and he met Mary Quant at art school). But, a singular point, Shirley was *finished* at Neuchâtel in

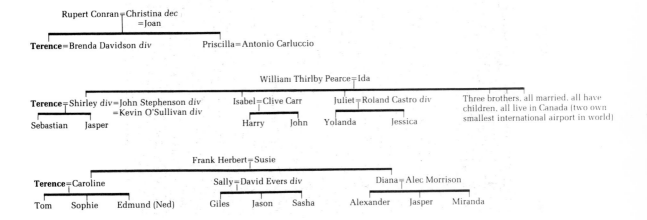

wanted to see the future. They shared the aesthetic of the Simple.

Terence and Shirley (the world still sees them as the Conrans though they have been divorced for twenty years and they were only married for eight) both went to private schools themselves – Bryanston for him, St Paul's for her – and both came from that kind of upper-middle class in flux that fuelled so much of the sixties. Terence Conran was Distressed Gentlefolk, Shirley was Home Counties plutocratic (her father had a dry-cleaning chain and ran a Roller). Neither school turns out

Switzerland. A point, one might say, of conflicting style. It came in handy, however, since *Lace* was plotted around a group of friends who meet at a Swiss finishing school in the late forties.

Among Shirley's contemporaries at the school in Neuchâtel was Jill Tweedie, the *Guardian's* thoughtful ex-columnist. From then on the CVs simply slam away like they're coming out of a telex. Terence worked on the Festival of Britain furniture, opened a restaurant (pine-boarded walls, quarry-tiled floor, cane-seated chairs ...) and then went seriously into furniture designing and making. By the early sixties he had a substantial factory in Norfolk. The first Habitat opened in March 1964, in Tottenham Court Road. Onward and upward.

Shirley crammed it in too. She moved from design-PR-ing to being the Conran *organiser* from 1955 on, doing the publicity, the exhibitions, the fabric division and the Conran textile design studio, staffed by the RCA, by 1958. And then – logical progression – *into media,* as Home Editor of the *Daily Mail* in 1962 and as the first Women's Editor of the *Observer* colour magazine. There she was, at the heart of colour consumerism, in at the beginning. And then, after some lean years post-divorce in the late sixties/early seventies, came *Superwoman,* 1975, which *charted* in the publishing lists as both hardback and Penguin No. 1s. In 1977, Shirley moved to Monte Carlo.

It was only in the mid-sixties, by which time they'd married (in 1955), had Sebastian and Jasper and parted, that the precise nature of the Conran talent became clear. No one had ever seen Conran as a stunningly original designer. Shirley wasn't a remarkable writer. They were both extremely competent. As *retailer* and *editor,* however, they were brilliant. They knew what was wanted, they responded, they *made it happen.* They understood the great art of *packaging,* of getting what marketing men call the 'mix' right, making a whole sensibility accessible all at once, quite painlessly. Terence's was an *editorial* skill; Shirley was always a retailer of ideas. It is beside the point to say the Habitat merchandise was hardly original, even in 1964, or that *Superwoman* and its successor *Futures* contained much that was neither new nor remarkable. Nor even to point out, like, say, the *Mail's* Lynda Lee-Potter, who appears to have a thing about Shirley, that she has used a lot of help. The Conrans had the initiatives and without them it wouldn't have got done. They gave their loyalists what was needed, in the right doses and at the right times.

The other packaging skill, of course, is making it look nice, understandable and inviting. As founder-Visuals they always understood presentation, that the right *context,* lighting and mood

## JASPER

Jasper Conran, 25, is a PERSONALITY. He's often touted as the best young English dress designer. Like the American successes Calvin Klein and Ralph Lauren, his clothes are described, ominously, as 'flattering', 'wearable', and sometimes 'classic'. He admires the simplicity of Chanel. Journalists love Jasper because he's articulate, precocious and funny, prematurely 40. (Whereas with most dress designers the conversation's a bit . . . limited.) Over the last five years, Jasper has been developed from cottage industry into an international label. He gives the people what they want.

Boy Jasper

could make you see something differently, make you feel better about the merchandise; that good art direction was worth the money. Hence the Habitat catalogue, now a book in its own right, and their instinctive understanding of publicity ...

These practical people made the very model of modern retailing and journalism geared to consumption. If there was a faint whiff of ideology around Terence's references to all those old design dicta of the thirties – after all Habitat did make the Bauhaus *happen* in England – and Shirley showed some interest in women's issues, it was, quite rightly, secondary to getting on with it. The Conrans haven't been run up sixties backwaters like some of their NW1 friends.

Conran uses his country house, Barton Court near Newbury, as a set for Habitat catalogue photography. It is the extreme expression of the style, extreme because of its over-scale, because it's got extras the Habitat buyers don't have. But it's not been decorated, Fowlerised, it isn't in the straight haute bourgeois mode. The reader can *identify*.

But the Conrans, Terence and his third wife Caroline, the cookery writer, and *their* children, don't, of course, have much in common with a social worker in Coventry. Shirley isn't really like the girl on the Sheffield *Telegraph*. They're richer, tougher, more metropolitan, better-connected. The Conrans are more *ramified* than you'd ever guess.

When the *News of the World* interviewed Shirley's boy Sebastian about his life as a punk-follower in 1977 he said he 'didn't believe in papers like the *News of the World*'. Sebastian's aunt, Shirley's sister Isabel, is married to Clive Carr, of the Park Lane Hotel family, the last surviving Carr director with Murdoch's News International. The Carrs used to own the *NOW*. There's more straight City/plutocratic there than the style reveals.

Conran's family, it is said, used to own land around Barton Court. Habitat has helped him recover it. Terence's sister Priscilla is the director of the Conran shop in Fulham Road as well as 'creative co-ordinator' of Habitat Mothercare PLC.

She is married to Antonio Carlucci, who runs the Conran-owned Neal Street Restaurant.

What the Conrans are doing *now* defines what's happened to a generation. When, for instance,

## SEBASTIAN

Sebastian Conran, 29, trained as an industrial designer, joined the product team of his father's 1982 acquisition, Mothercare, last spring, where he works under creative director John Stephenson (see family tree) and creative co-ordinator Priscilla Carluccio (ditto). Sebastian came up through Bryanston, punk (he was a Clash roadie) and mainstream design – working at Conran competitor, Wolff Olins.

Conran told Wilfrid De'Ath in *The Times* that he now 'saw the point' of Chippendale, it spoke volumes, not just about aesthetics, but about the Conran world-view, about a generation's certainties.

Meanwhile, Terence is looking more bankerly, more *bankable* than ever. Shorter hair, good suits, Skone & Poulsen shoes. And when Shirley set out to produce an 'international' airport novel in the Krantz-Susann mode – the style a perfect pastiche, the content the optimal package (money, movie stars, Arab princes, roman-à-clef) – she showed a gamesman's determination to master the commercial form. After *Superwoman*, she simply had to

## THE BOILERHOUSE

The Conran-financed museumette of industrial design, at present inside the V & A, set the seal on Conran's design-establishment legitimacy. In the early sixties, Conran's membership of the Society of Industrial Designers was withdrawn in a dispute over his 'advertising' for business. And his fellow designers have occasionally sniped about his lack of originality, his business methods, etc. But the launching of the Boilerhouse in 1981 (under director Stephen Bayley) took Conran into the upper air.

make the big kill. There's no turning back. Jasper Conran is almost couture. He makes clothes for the Princess of Wales. He lives in Primrose Hill. 'I'm second-generation NW1,' he says.

In *Nineteen Eighty-Four*, a book every generation of teenagers reads, Winston Smith is betrayed, not under the spreading chestnut tree, but in Prole Town. Prole Town is the area that lies outside the compound, the planners' city. In Prole Town, where the traditional urban peasants free-range, Smith finds a subversive junk shop, where things *are the way they were*, and the old proprietor says subversive things like, 'Who cares about genuine antiques nowadays – even the few that are left?' and confirms his suspicions of a different life, a different language, outside the world of rewritten histories and double-plus ungood. The shop is, of course, a *front* for the system, designed to ensnare

# F·A·N·T·A·S·I·A
# O·N  A  T·H·E·M·E  P·A·R·K

the sentimental Winstons of life; the old proprietor is an *agent provocateur* and the whole place is under constant electronic surveillance. Winston gets hauled in for re-education pretty soon.

On 19 June 1980 the reconstructed Covent Garden market – formerly the old fruit and vegetable building – opened with tremendous coverage as London's first permanent late-night shopping centre. It is, strictly speaking, an upmarket *shopping leisure development,* a new shopping *mall* artfully shoehorned into an old building of character. The first advertising read 'London's new historic shopping experience'.

The production values are ordered with great concern for authenticity; there are even mandatory regulations about the retention and restoration of period features inside the tenant shops – fancy ironwork and suchlike. There are, however, some odd and interesting things to be observed –

Dreaming spires of the Theme Age: Cinderella's castle in Disneyworld

the lanterns outside, made to a traditional pattern, are glazed in plastic, the modern sprinkler system is fairly naked and the cash registers are of the newest kind, meaning several are generically *computer terminals*. There is something about the new/old Covent Garden market that reminds one of such stage-craft as the reconstructed shopfronts in museums like the Museum of London or the V & A or the redone bits of Williamsburg or Boston, and also, one has to say, of Disney World in Florida. All this reflects the very peculiar commercial/social character of the new Covent Garden area as a whole. If you look at the kinds of businesses that now predominate round there – architects, advertising agencies, graphic designers and design consultants, illustrators and every other kind of commercial designer and environmental rearranger possible – and the facilities –

*Left* Faneuil Hall, Boston: refurbished shopping mall theme park

*Below right* Pier 39, Fisherman's Wharf, San Francisco, USA

*Below* Covent Garden central market building: a land fit for designers to live in. Note the characteristic light fittings

Covent Garden is one vast designers' world, with Penhaligon's doing the Cinderella's castle job, as a Victorian scented bower (scent package designs by Michael Peters) and the Club Kids – those strange art-school *manqué* fantasists who'd gone from neon and Lycra to full-tilt period fantasy and Hard Times in a few years – as the character extras. Covent Garden is clearly the newest of a series of new urban theme parks: areas planned, reconstructed, laid on, for total experience.

After the old market went and the planning fuss died down, Covent Garden was systematically developed away from 'traditional' industry or commerce and into the 'being' professions – life to be seen and consumed for itself. This is why the shops in the new market are so weird – they are theme shops, designed to suit a very modern sensibility: a new kind of touristic experience. There are, of course, all kinds of specialist shops – crafts and antiques and health foods and esoterica – servicing a variety of specialist tastes, but a great many have in common the intent to be authentic and old-fashioned, hence Thornton's chocolates – an old-established family firm, and Peelers – 'a brasserie/restaurant decorated on police themes and colours' with a menu 'based on traditional English food'. Fenn's is 'a marvellously old-fashioned butcher' and Fern's 'one of London's grand old coffee shops', and so on. Culpeper and Elizabeth David and Cranks, and antique shops of a certain sort – dolls and old newspapers and movie memorabilia – are fragments of the past, the natural, the naïve, scrupulously assembled and reconstructed as references, accessories, sign language.

Covent Garden is a good example of the com-

themed restaurants and wine bars which have *all been designed* – you realise that Covent Garden is the tip, the harbinger of the modern world, of real-life theme parks.

Everybody in Covent Garden, consciously or not, is doing their bit in the *grand tableau* – their contribution to what Walt Disney called 'imagineering' – the professional dreaming up and executing of three-dimensional fantasies. The new

mercially successful consolidation of enthusiasms – the enthusiasms and aesthetics of the design types who create, endorse and consume today's theme parks, the art-directed worlds where everything is designed. The social process that Covent Garden represents pulls together two key, and apparently opposed, trends of the last twenty years – urban planning and speculative leisure development, much of it inspired by the extraordinary examples from America, and particularly by Walt Disney.

Disney invented the theme park, a totally new kind of entertainment, at Disneyland, California in 1955. Disneyland was – sensibly enough for the creation of a man who had made his fortune in animated movies – out of the movies and into 3D. A multi-media fantasy environment that took every American peasant's dream – from Cinderella's castle, to the Future, to the quintessential nineteenth-century Main Street that never was – and made it flesh on a plot twice as big as Hyde Park. It was kitsch, it was spectacular; the technology, the management skills were faultless; and it was an enormous commercial success over precisely the period that movies started to decline. Disneyland, unlike traditional amusement parks of the Southend or Coney Island variety, was totally planned – safe, clean, sequential and thematic, a total experience designed by 'imagineers', another Disney word. Intellectuals sneered at the fibrous plaster and 'plastic', the 'inauthenticity', the cuteness; were satirical, or indeed, sometimes, saw in it a sinister right-wing plot to enslave the proles. In particular, early architects derided the lack of architectural courage. The proles – or rather America's post-prole 'middle class' in its Chevies – kept on coming, in their millions. By 1972, when the Disney Corporation (Walt died in 1966) opened Walt Disney World at Orlando, Florida (a vast new town twice the size of Manhattan excavated out of the Florida swamp at a cost at least double that of any real new towns – something like $400 million start-up), attitudes had changed.

It had to be admitted then that Walt had been, as the Disney PR had claimed all along, a visionary.

The order of the technological and other innovations, the sheer scale of the project and, above all, the shift in high-culture tastes, meant the reaction was different. Architects – by the late seventies at least – were saying they found Disneyland and Disney World *fun* and seminal. Literary intellectuals of the Frenchified kind saw in it a degraded Utopia, full of signs and meaning. In particular, the new technology – of total planning from below ground up – was fascinating. Disney World was built around innovative service and computer sub-systems planned into one vast basement that had town planners green with envy. Back-stage at Disney World was as exciting as the display. Real life, so they said, could learn from Disney World. And above ground the scale, the effects, the robotics, the dancing bears, the exotic birds controlled by computer, were all incredible, even if the vision was wearing a bit thin and the obsessive child-orientation of the organisation becoming a little out of step with the times.

The critical praise indicated just two things: that Disney was already just a bit out of date and that we, the people, the little British people, would get something of the kind soon. Throughout the seventies English theme parks were planned by leisure conglomerates of the Mecca/EMI variety, and foundered – as such things do in conglomerates – on economic stop-go. EMI were going to do one on the site of the Battersea Funfair – it sounded very Southend – and Mecca planned a thousand-acre 'Merrie England' in Staffordshire. Something called the Romm Doulton Organisation planned to open the old Agricultural Hall in Islington, as a 'Dickens World', but that apparently aborted too, though they continued to talk engagingly of their 'Sherwood Forest' scheme.

What we actually have, however, are Thorpe Park at Staines and the Palladium Cellars. Both are essentially pre-Disney in conception and execution – neither a full-tilt themed experience. But while the Palladium Cellars, a *tableau* partly *vivant*, mainly wax, is a rather effective development of the Tussaud formula put on by a proper movie showman – Michael Carreras from the Hammer Horror family – Thorpe Park, which calls itself 'Britain's first theme park', is both pallid and tacky as only a certain kind of British leisure enterprise can be. Thorpe Park, which sits around a lake (a filled gravel pit) near Staines, is a diversification of a building-product manufacturing group called Ready Mixed Concrete. Thorpe Park does not raise questions about the nature of the modern world, but rather about the nature of British industry. It is deeply inhibited, British fifties provincial, a desultory cluster of provincial museum exhibits and inaccurate-looking reconstructions dotted around some green fields near a motorway, rather like early Heathrow. But certainly not a fantasy world. We are unlikely to get *the real thing* until one of the American operators opens here (cf McDonald's, etc), and it looks as though Disney would rather do a joint venture with Japan than the UK.

Theming and stage-craft also had an odd effect on the traditional world of museums. The really big attendances in museums and galleries over the last twenty years came from the stagey blockbuster exhibitions, starting with Richard Buckle's 'Diaghilev' show of 1954 which went from the Edinburgh festival to Forbes House in Halkin Street, SW1, where costumes moved in fanned air scented with Guerlain Mitsouko (and a generation of aesthetes learned to refer to the top-right-hand corner of Belgrave Square as 'past Diaghilev'). The highpoint was probably the Tutankhamun exhibition at the British Museum in 1972. All these exhibitions, drawing on various multi-media tricks from the stage, video, hippyland happenings, etc., encouraged a taste for events, *theming*, lifestyles and experiences, that wasn't easily satisfied by traditional museum display techniques (indeed the current debate about what museums are *for* has been largely provoked by the public voting with its feet for the themed exhibitions).

The other ideal setting for theming was the modern restaurants, where the diners, the staff, the Life made the cabaret, where the atmosphere and clientele were *planned in*, because the opening ('Who's covering this party?') had a PR and a cast list. Thus you got not show-business restaurants but 'show-business restaurants'. The food was an accessory to the theme and the criteria for judgement were new ones; did the food go with the art direction? Thus Joe Allen, with its bar and unrendered walls and check cloths and blackboard menu, is Upper West Side Stage World – at a stroke. The new Sheekey's is more old-fashioned than the old one (Edwardian Stage-Door Johnny World), and folk table-hopped in the first epic PR Golden Days of Langan's Brasserie in late 1976 (Slightly Neo-Decadent Fashion World).

During the sixties and seventies, a new kind of theme park was emerging across the world: the gentrified change-of-use *quartier*, once plebeian or industrial in the real world, made over to the creative leisure life, the world of *taste*. In these places, a certain life is lived, a certain life *laid on*; bits of the past, of small plebeian businesses, of trades, of *characters* are retained to give atmosphere, while the essential class, ownership and occupational base changes out of sight.

These developments tend to be bound up with notions of urban renewal, planning participation and the like, but in practice usually favour a certain kind of new middle-class person, the non-specific or commercial creative. Graphic designers and female photojournalists aside, this class, especially in America, is now quite a large minority with a high disposable income and an inclination towards vaguely artistic forms of consumption, such as eating in *themed* restaurants (post-hippy vegetarian, French and English Provincial, etc.) and wine bars. The loft life of SoHo, the quintessential artists' colony theme park in New York, is precisely this. SoHo is thirty-five blocks of hundred-year-old loft buildings – warehouses – just north of Wall Street in lower Manhattan, self-consciously the first mixed residential, commercial and industrial area since New York was 'zoned' in the early 1900s. SoHo has *character*. It is also increasingly expensive, and poor artistic types cannot afford to live there. The main activity in SoHo is more on the conceptual consumption side, the main sensibility the remodelled. Victorian industrial, the main retailing base, art galleries. There are fifty galleries and most of them appear to be selling hyper-realistic pictures of fifties cars in vast whitewashed rooms with wooden floors.

SoHo's other occupation is *interior decoration*, building character into the $20,000 lofts. The SoHo type of architectural restoration change-of-use formula has been applied in a number of downtown areas of character, like Old Montreal, and the Cannery and Ghirardelli Square in San Francisco and Faneuil Hall in Boston, which is astonishingly similar to the redeveloped Covent Garden market. And everywhere you get this same mix of occupations and shops and sensibilities, and the complete disappearance of the original functional base of the place – the heavy industry, the ordinary shops, to be replaced by the funky middle-class tourist, living for the real thing. The American search for the authentic is easy to satirise, but it's also easy to miss the importance of these areas as social laboratories, test-driving ways of life for the mainstream. The way of life that SoHo celebrates is the one you find in all those

movies of self-realisation at the age of 32, like *Girlfriends*. This kind of redevelopment (usually commercial at heart despite its public relations) tends to work commercially. That is, to be more responsive to market forces than the most participative socialist planning. Above all it makes allowance for the fact that modern middle-class Americans live for experience, and that leisure – depression or not – remains their main growth industry.

One American usage has always fascinated me. Americans of a certain kind say 'unreconstructed' of a thing that is merely *real*. The American expectation is that a thing *will* have been reconstructed, decorated, faked up, fiddled about with, rethought, redone. This places a heavy burden on the real thing as a symbol of another life. Perhaps this explains Pet Rocks. It certainly explains the active search for a different order of experience and stimulation, a life that looks the part, and it is certainly why Americans are best at theme parks proper, and first off the mark in the theme park

Brent Cross: early sixties-style late-seventies Astrodome shopping mall in North London

development of Downtown. Whether the theme park principle has anything to offer more ordinary kinds of planning is less clear – save the recognition that people respond to being on stage in a setting and living by rules of dramaturgy.

Many 'serious' planners are suspicious of the theme park approach – they see it as ersatz, commercially opportunistic, short-term and elitist, essentially not serious as a way of solving urban problems. The signs are, however, that some serious planners and architects have seen the Disneylands and SoHos as harbinger developments, and during a crisis in planning the idea of cosy architecture with period themes, of traditional (kitsch) street patterns, of the selective use of reconstructed period elements, even of outright fakery ('judicious restoration and infill') are arousing some interest. Certainly the language of the commercial imagineers must be fascinating – and faintly alarming – to planners with social science backgrounds. The language of social control and management crops up all the time. I found one group of theme park consultants who loved talking about 'pulling strings'. Another talks of 'theatre' in which 'guests also have roles to play'. The ultimate theme park fantasy is Michael Crichton's movie *Westworld*. Cheaply made in 1973, *Westworld* posits the definitive theme park, a computer-based experience holiday where the traveller enters Westworld (cowboys) – or Roman World or Medieval World – and takes experience one step further; *screw* robots . . . *fight* them . . . *kill* them. Westworld sets up for the visitor a kind of OK Corral gunfight with a robotic villain which he'll win every time. It goes wrong, however; the robots get a screw loose and start killing the guests. *Westworld* works at a fairly straightforward thriller level. The hardware and the special effects are what matter and the implications aren't laid on too heavily. But it's an important film, irrespective of quality, because it has caught a raft of contemporary American myths and aspirations in an uncommonly predictive way – the lifestyle of tourist as Hero.

The Trocadero, Piccadilly Circus leisure centre, incorporates Guinness Records world

Bringing out the girls at
the Reform Club: the one
in front has got the hang
of it

## D·E·S·I·G·N·T·I·M·E

# V·I·C·T·O·R·I·A·N   V·A·L·U·E·S

At the Victorian Society's Grand Victorian Ball the revellers – Hussars and Souls and hostesses and the odd Diamond Lil – fitted their costumes better than ever. The mood was more High Victorian then Mid – Nicola Bayley in her Grisi garland stood out against a style that was thrusting towards the 1890s – even the Edwardian Imperial and Sargent. They had caught the mood; Victorian values – High Victorian values particularly – were not to be laughed at in 1984 and particularly not in the Fine Art ghetto. In 1983 the sale-room record for a Victorian painting was broken and three pictures sold for over half a million: first Richard Dadd's *Oberon and Titania* (£550,000 including premium); then Tissot's *Garden Bench* (£561,000 including premium) and finally Millais's *Proscribed Royalist* (£842,400 including premium). And around Christmas everybody had wind of the story that Owen Edgar of West Halkin Street had sold Alma-Tadema's Hollywood-marbleous *Baths of Caracalla* for a million pounds – and since then about a dozen Tademas have fetched that price. In particular, it seemed that the market was taking most of the Eminents – those knighted RAs, the Melbury Road Masters, the St John's Wood mob, at their contemporary valuation. While any 'good' Victorian went well, the big names went super well. *The Eminent Victorians were being reinstated.* Lord Leighton to you, sonny, Sir John Millais, Sir Lawrence Alma-

Tadema, each had his dealer, his scholar, his *catalogue raisonné*. They were certainly not *amusing*; you don't pay a million for an amusing picture. And there is more to come; now the sixteen-year retreat from inhibition about the Victorianness of Victorian painters has finally reached home. In making merely respectable prices some second-league 'good' (ie well-made) Victorian pictures are still selling well below their original prices in 1980 values. There is ground to make up. We're talking about pictures that made, oh, up to £10,000 then (with the reproduction rights that made nineteenth-century pop stars from major artists), Millais reckoned to knock up £35,000 a year in his golden days, with income tax at 1d in the pound.

There was once a dismal little calculation made for some year in the late seventies that showed something like twenty British-based *recording artistes* had personal incomes of a million or more. *Well*, they had nothing on the artist-knights who were pop stars and Clive Sinclair in one go. Only novelists and poets came close. The Eminents, after all, worked for reproduction, and engravings from their work went via 'prints', novels and history books into every Pooter villa – and socially well below – in Victorian Britain. They shaped the way generations of English people saw the world, up until at least the last war. Seven million saw Holman Hunt's *Light of the World* when the Fine Art Society toured it around the Empire from 1905–7.

And now there is a game they play in the mile around Bond Street and St James's which is, what would happen if one of the two Victorian masterpieces – the acknowledged copper-bottomed ones

*Left* Lord Leighton's *Flaming June* (currently in *Puerto Rico!*) ... 'Oh, at least a three/four million picture for sure ...'

*Right* Tissot's *Garden Bench*: doomed idyll with perfect production values, £561,000

– were to hit the market? People in the business constantly come up with this one – what if Leighton's *Flaming June* or Ford Madox Brown's *Work* were actually in the sale-rooms ... 'Oh, a three/four million picture for sure ...'

In 1963 Jeremy Maas, whose superbly produced *Victorian Painters* marked the start of the move in 1969, sold *Flaming June* for £2,000. It was wildly expensive then. Friends and rivals were astonished that Maas had parlayed a Leighton up to there. Those great soapy classicists with their De Mille movie sets and their wispy titillation, you couldn't give them away. Regularly – through from the thirties to the early sixties – major Victorians who sold for thousands then, and sell for tens and hundreds of thousands now, could be picked up for a few hundred or less. Consider, if only for its *neatness*, the following: at Christie's in

1927 Sir George Clausen's *Allotment Gardens* fetched £350; in 1937, £35; in 1977, £3,500; in 1987? In the wilderness years Victorian pictures – like Victorian architecture – were a tipple for a particular type of clever perverse sensibility – Waugh, Betjeman and Osbert Lancaster all did their bit. After the war there came the rush of chi-chi Victorian and Edwardian pastiche of the late forties. Button-back chairs and 'Victoriana' got going then with all the cottage and fairground looks, the precursors of the mid-sixties Portobello Great Gear Pop Victoriana. Pop-Vic, like the hippie pash for the Pre-Raphaelites, was a transitional thing. Pop-Vic was equivocal, it selected commercial nineteenth-century stuff because its ludicrous blandishments could be made to look funny.

The people of NW1 could rise above nineteenth-century capitalism – stuffed and mounted

– in an enamel sign or corset advertising. Something of this feeling was behind the ubiquitous sixties Lord Kitchener poster reprint.

The Pre-Raphaelites were hair and haberdashery for the hippies but this kind of endorsement (gee, I love the purple clothes you wear and the way the sunlight plays upon your hair) helped make the Pre-Raphaelites visible – a Waterhouse, *Hylas and the Nymphs*, for instance, was an immensely popular bed-sit poster in the late sixties. Original or acid pastiche Pre-Raphaelitism ended up on a lot of record covers. Nonetheless much of the serious critical endorsement came from the snobbish idea that the Pre-Raphaelites were somehow un-Victorian – fantastical and hence international, influencing the French Symbolists and making a direct statement to the young troubadour folk and all that. It helped to think of them in terms of Art Rebel. Only in the Seventies did the Victorianness of Victorian Art start to make a direct appeal. Only in 1969 did Jeremy Maas dare call an exhibition at his gallery 'Victorian' just straight out. Hippie may have helped but it was the retreat from hippie over the seventies that precisely paralleled the changes in attitudes towards Victorian painting in general and its surprisingly steady fourteen-year price rise. Other seventies casualties, not unrelated, were Freud, the Modern Movement in architecture, and finally, in 1979, the Labour Party.

The shift in attitudes on a host of apparently unrelated fronts made it possible to take the most Victorian of Victorian Art, the 'genre' painters and the later classicists, seriously. The increasing large format Art Paperback industry showed how gorgeous some of these things could look to generations that had never heard of Herbert Read or Roger Fry. And of course the Art Market needed the Victorians, as the standard millionaires' tipples – the Impressionists particularly – because unaffordable and unavailable (as Institutions bought them), so only second-rank pictures sold at silly prices. Kip Forbes, son of *Forbes* magazine, started his Victorian collection in Old Battersea House, in the early seventies, on the premise that he could buy the best for the price of a second-rate Pissarro.

Mrs Thatcher no doubt thinks Art's a Fart and would tell you so but she admires a well-made English thing with a high polish, as we saw on her guided tour of 10 Downing Street. Her views on nineteenth-century art are not recorded but you feel she could easily find something to her taste. High Victorian, like Alma-Tadema's french-polished marble baths (even if they did pander to Denis a bit much), was *made* for big new money. It shouts (*pace* William Davis) 'It's no sin to be rich'. The chivalric pictures have Falklands Factor in Spades, the Orientalists have echoes of Empire. Other earlier work is resonant with the Grantham thirties self-help aesthetic, and the *family* is celebrated in pictures right through the reign. The nineteenth century was the British century. The kind of High Victorian – and, increasingly, Edwardian – Art that is fashionable now across Europe – Salon Painting, Artistes pompiers (they're even starting to call it *Victorian* in France and Germany) hits the Thatcher Kohl mood exactly.

There is now the simple recognition that painting like this is a lost craft. No one will ever do years of the Royal Academy Schools again – the endless weeks of *drapery sketches*, the grind years of regular portraiture, the six-day week in the St John's Wood studio; Alma-Tadema's hundreds of notebooks of classical detail. The best Victorian painting is incredibly well-made – at the *object* level. The best later Victorians, many of whom pottered on almost into the twenties, were the last generation to work that way. It is now as remote from *Art Education* as Islamic Fundamentalism. You don't need an elaborate biographical scam or an Art Theory to fancy a good Victorian picture –

there it is, acres of french-polished oil with beautiful women and hand-tooled detail (oh, the *work* in it, as the mockers used to say) and Classical isn't hackneyed if you didn't go to Portheboys Hall.

The people, of course, never really deserted representational art – they took a line of latter-day Landseers and Leightons like Peter Scott and the Elephant Man or Tretchikhoff's *Green Girl*, right through the century, only buying Modern Art when it took the form of cute little string cat's-cradles mounted on velvet for under a fiver at the general store. *Modern Art*, they discerned, was a source of cheap and amusing knick-knacks but it made no sense to pay good money for it.

**1918** Dark days, Lytton Strachey (tall, 'bent as sloppy asparagus') knocks the horsehair out of *Eminent Victorians*.

**1919** Victorian pioneer, Harry Goodhart-Rendel (guardsman, whizz on military drill, 'astrakhan coat and eyeglass') writes the first serious article on V buildings. 'The father of us all,' said Kenneth Clark.

**1920** Frying tonight. Bloomsberries sizzling because young smarties start pulling mid-V furniture out of the attic. Roger Fry has fear of mahogany in *Vision & Design* (famous essay: 'The Ottoman and the Whatnot').

**1922** Victoriana an Oxford undergraduate joke. In *Brideshead Revisited* Sebastian Flyte pix Vix ('a harmonium in a Gothic case, an elephant's foot waste-paper basket, a dome of waxed fruit, two disproportionately large Sèvres vases, framed drawings by Daumier'). Charles Ryder sells his Omega screen.

**1923** First Victorian fancy-dress party given by the Hypocrites Club (at house in St Aldate's, Oxford). Décor by Oliver Messel (imitation Landseer still-lifes suspended from ceiling, scenes from V history painted on walls). Harold Acton (who collects artificial fruit and flowers, lumps of glass, paper-weights) wears military uniform, Robert Byron (wrote *The Road to Oxiana*) flashes in as the Widow of Windsor (his resemblance to old Queen V very striking).

**1923** Hollywood rescues Dickens (Child Coogan stars in *Oliver Twist*).

**1924** Oxford Proctors ban 1840s Exhibition ('a bevy of stuffed parrots and a spinster built of shells') planned at Merton by Byron, Acton and Evelyn Waugh ('a little gnome in checks'). (Then a dome of wax fruit cost 10d, a Staffordshire figure 1s, a wool picture £1.) Catalogue to have introduction by surprise defector Lytton Strachey.

**1926** Waugh privately prints PRB: *An Essay on the Pre-Raphaelite Brotherhood* (goitre-ing with intent). Ding-dong Clive Bell *hates* the PRB ('a smear which to this day defiles British painting').

**1927** Widow of Windsor (Robert Byron again) streaks into a London party. (Then all vile bodies wore fancy dress.)

**1928** Waugh presses on with *William Rossetti* (£50 advance for Duckworth). Kenneth Clark publishes *The Gothic Revival* (idea suggested by C.F., yet another Bell who expected 'a sort of satire'. Very surprised).

**1930** Aldous Huxley savages Little Nell (in *Vulgarity in Literature*). Please Leavis alone.

**1932** John Rothenstein (the Uncle Jasper of V painting) barnstorms on with *Nineteenth-Century Painting* (very abusive). Influences British art-gallery directors well into the sixties. Provincial horror stories (Leeds City Art Gallery wouldn't lend V pictures in case they gave the gallery 'a bad reputation'). Only old-fashioned northern magnates loyal to Pre-Raphaelite pictures ('a lovely sunset floosh').

**1932** Centenary Burne-Jones Exhibition at the Tate (a quiet affair).

**1934** Centenary William Morris Exhibition at the V&A (another quiet affair).

**1936** The Crystal Palace burns down 30 Nov to 1

Dec. Streets of Sydenham run with molten glass ('a real calamity,' says *The Times*). Linked with Abdication crisis as the end of Victorian values (again).

**1937** Old snap books start here. Peter Quennell (Britain's most obscure famous critic) publishes *Victorian Panorama* (life and fashion in *real* V photographs).

**1938** Osbert Lancaster (handle-bar moustache, 'draws like friendly viper') publishes *Pillar to Post*. Coins seven types of V building, including Municipal Gothic, Pont Street Dutch, Public-House Classic, Scottish Baronial ('minimum of comfort with maximum of expense').

**1939** Cecil Beaton whisked to Palace (July) to photograph the Queen in her 'dew-spangled' Hartnell crinolines. ('Just like a Winterhalter painting!' squeaks attendant.) For evening, clever Queen Mum stays with Winterhalter look ever since. (Winterhalter did for crowned heads what Landseer did for stags. Made even VR wait because he was 'busy painting Poles and Russians'.)

**1940** Michael Sadleir (publisher of K. Clark, Trollope expert) writes *Fanny by Gaslight*, his most famous neo-V novel. (Fanny is Granny of *The French Lieutenant's Woman*.)

**1950** Campaign for Real Pubs. Hubert de Cronin Hastings (dotty genius, proprietor of the Architectural Press) builds Victorian gin palace ('The Bride of Denmark') in basement of his Queen Anne's Gate offices. Lord Moyne contributes stuffed lion (hindquarters had to be unstuffed and rolled up to get into glass case).

**1951** Greenhouse-sized model of Crystal Palace on show at Festival of Britain (background blasts of

The Queen Mother (then Queen)
in her 'dew-spangled' Hartnell
Winterhalter crinoline, July 1939

Hallelujah Chorus and *Zadok the Priest*). You climbed into it from a ladder.

**1952** Major turning point. Peter Floud puts on Victorian and Edwardian Decorative Arts exhibition at V&A. Inspires new V collecting mania (particularly in top collectors of the sixties, Charles and Lavinia Handley-Read).

**1954** American prof (Henry-Russell Hitchcock) makes useful list of V buildings (*Early Victorian Architecture in Britain*). All done from top of bus.

**1955** William Morris Society founded (wallpaper designer, Socialist agitator, 'liked being taken for a sea-captain').

**1957 Victorian Society (Vixoc) founded** ('with knockout Martinis') by Lady Rosse at 18 Stafford Terrace (now Linley Sambourne House, open to public). It was 5 Nov ('Guy Fawkes rockets outside and that poor dog, Little Lemon, was going round in Sputnik II'). New Vix included Lord Rosse, Oliver Messel, John Piper, James and John Pope-Hennessy, Rosamond Lehmann, Lord Esher, Robert Harling, John Fowler, James Lees-Milne, Thomas Pakenham, Mark Girouard and Peter Clarke (founder of the famous Vixoc walks).

**1960** Jeremy Maas opens his gallery in Clifford Street, W1 (staarts putting V aart on the maap).

**1961-62** British Rail (the Villain) pushes finely chiselled Euston Station (the Hero) in path of an express train. Vixoc takes its first test case to Cabinet level. PM (Harold Macmillan) washes his hands of the Euston Arch (now Earl of Stockton-and-Darlington-Railway).

**1963** Nikolaus Pevsner ('the Dok') becomes Chairman of Vixoc. Gives it academic teeth ('From heart of Mittel-Europ, I make der little trip, To show these English Dummkopfs, Some echt-Deutsch scholarship'). Forbids use of word 'Victoriana' (still non-U for *proper* Vix).

**1968** New bronze age: Peyton Skipworth digs up V sculpture (puts on British Sculpture 1850–14 at Fine Art Society, New Bond Street, W1). Includes Lord Leighton's *Athlete Wrestling with a Python*. ('Metal-work and bric-à-brac,' says the *Observer*).

**1969** Now is the Winterhalter of our content (Christie's opens department of V paintings).

**1970** John Betjeman ('warm, mysterious force behind the V revival') brings love of V buildings to suburban man (BBC-TV series, 'Victorian Architects and Architecture'). Brilliant on box (and *Private Eye's* original Nooks & Corners man).

**1971** Sotheby's founds department of V pix.

**1973** Richard Dadd Exhibition at the Tate (nice, loopy fairy painter who murdered his father). Big hit with hippies. (The seventies went exhibition mad: eight major shows on V subjects from 1971 to '78 and *hundreds and hundreds* of books.)

**1979** Christopher Wood opens gallery in Motcomb Street, SW1.

**1980s** Vix on top.

**1983** Furniture: Auberon Waugh sells Burges cabinet for £45,000. Pre-Raphaelite exhibition at the Tate.

**1984** *The Proscribed Royalist* by Millais sold for £842,400 (one of the highest prices ever paid for a V painting).

Jeremy Maas with a nice piece

Millais' *Proscribed Royalist*: one of your history book favourites for just £842,400

For the man with the child in his eyes – KicKers®! Big laces, big eyelets, big soles, dinky feet

## B·A·B·Y·T·I·M·E
# A·N·O·R·E·X·I·A   O·

The shoe's the thing in Babyland – soft shoes, sweet bounce of youth, every kind of soft shoe there ever was: Kickers; those black Chinese cloth slippers; dinky little baseball boots; Olaf Daughters; Clarks' trad' daisy sandals (rerun in bright colours); those home-made radical feminist pram shoes you buy in Camden Lock; little plastic pumps; sneakers; jellies. Anything with a soft sole and an alternative upper (not hard *chrome* leather as they call it in the trade).

The Baby people always wear soft shoes; shoes that don't stamp and march and clack up the stairs or make any of those sexist sounds. Shoes that don't have to be bulled up with Kiwi. Coloured shoes, particularly in the approved Babyland primaries: emerald (big with feminists); scarlet (hopeful boy journalists 1976); yellow (play-power/street theatre leftover). And pastels: pink for cute girls, pale blue for winsome wimps.

But the great Babytime story is the Kicker. The rise and fall of the Kicker is roughly conterminous with the second half of the Babytime – i.e. 1974–79. Kickers started off as shoes for foreign-French-babies and ended up, in the late seventies, selling more to Big Babies all over England. They were cute, they had *cachet*. In certain provincial milieux in the seventies a pair of *real* Kickers was like having real Levis in Omsk.

The basic Kicker was a five-year-old's bootee – a *bottine* – just scaled up. They were too delicious – Kickers were instant anorexia. Once on, the gonads shrank. How could those jolly coloured snub toes, those soft white-ridged soles mean anything but Bright Eyes ... the man with the child in his eyes.

Well la di dah: we've got a right one here. Mo – Little Mo because she's probably five eleven – is crisp, bright, ageless, skinny, though you assume some of the conventional equipment underneath her oversized pink denim all-in-one. The trouser cuffs are rolled up to mid-calf and she's got short pink socks – little girl's fifties socks – inside her button and bar pink canvas sneakers. She's got a big brown *Just William* satchel with a sticker of Rupert Bear on it over one shoulder. This, strictly, is her briefcase. Her bag is a child's miniature Mickey Mouse suitcase. On her lapels there's a collection of badges – Vice-Head Girl in enamel, an aeroplane cut from sheet acrylic, a round one saying 'I am 9' – 36 actually. Her hair is flattened in the middle by two pink pearlised plastic barettes, but flares out, blonde frizz, to the sides. On top she's got a scarlet bobbled cardi knitted from a 1978 Patricia Roberts pattern.

Mo is unmarried, childless. She threw Paul out when he lost his job and started to live on her in her little Barnsbury end-of-terrace conversion. He never knew what hit him. Mo talks bright high-pitched Babytalk – a chirpy chirpy cheep cheep whimsy, full of doggies and must-have-a-tinkle and early children's book mock-pompous – but she's the fastest gun alive on a contract, the very devil on the bottom line. She *is* headgirl – merchandise and design director for a chain of

Those tiny happy feet

The nursery tea table: pandas, toucans, Robertson gollies, postbox, thirties motor – every teapot that ever there was is gathered here together because today's the day the babytimers have their pic-nic

Sally of Sally's Own stall sells hand-knitted jumpers featuring froggies and other gambolling playmates. Sally wears bow in hair, sandals, stripey socks, 'dice' necklace and Mickey Mouse watch whose hands tell the time – 5 o'clock, time for tea at Sally's house with 1000 frogs

BABYTIME (ANOREXIA OF THE SOUL)

children's stores. Art school made good. She *hated* her mother, she hated every day of her fifties childhood in Luton, Beds.

Babytime was, roughly, from 1968 to 1980: a magic time when thousands of adult, sane, bourgeois men and women aspired to Babyhood. The man with the child in his eyes, Kickers on his feet and dungarees round the rest, walked the land, grown women in short socks at his side. They lived in a new primary and pastels Baby-land, a land where time stood still, and forged a new Babystyle. In all the big Western cities – but especially in London and New York – they made this extraordinary jump through the looking-glass.

Far beyond the *naïve*, the Marie Antoinette, the miraculous preservation, beyond even the per-petual teenage sunlight and into – pre-puberty. Innocent legs in short socks, hairless hands on the Sturmey Archer gearchange. The children of the Clarks daisy sandals or the Start-Rite kids walking down that rainbow road. A kitsch version of fifties childhood, remade for grown men and women who'd smoked and drunk and done drugs and done *it* and everything (Babytimers liked Baby-talking about sex). Sweet bounce of youth. The Babytimers weren't, you understand, just like the rest of mankind wanting to hang on to the Sex Prime with face-lifts and hair-pieces and all that familiar, understandable stuff. They wanted something astonishing – Second Childhood.

In this dawn of mass paedophilia, grown-ups stole the children's clothes. The kids didn't want them anyway. Tiny Brooke Shields and Jodie Fosters, miniature Travoltas and baby skinheads – the Mini-Pops – wanted designer jeans and glit-tery boob tubes, designer sportswear and leather blousons, not ankle socks and flannel shorts and Fairisles. Sense of period isn't very big with 10-year-olds. But the Babytime clothes were right for The Life which was about getting into yourself somehow or other. All the kiddie-related ideas which'd been hanging around since popular psycho-analysis started, became major gimmicky things in themselves. And some of the biggest products were all about going back. 'Rebirthing' and 'primal screaming' – never really big *here*, of

course – were about redemption and reverse initiation. John Lennon – in his later years a classi-cal Babytimer – actually enacted his primal screaming on record. Going Back. And of course anorexia really got going in the seventies – every-where – so by the end of the decade we all knew it was a Babytime phenomenon; part of the Peter Pan syndrome.

What happened was that the Babytimers were the front runners in the first generation ever to deny the life-cycle: marriage, commitment, baby-making. Hell no, we won't go – how could babies make babies, commit themselves to an irrelevant institution (remember people actually said those things, less than ten years ago . . .)? They weren't ready. You could be a student into your thirties. Women in what *Cosmopolitan*'s presentation to advertisers called the Freedom Years – 18 to 25 and more – could defer babies easily. Life's Club 18–30 – which became in practice 18–45 as the net went wider – extended the definition of teenage enormously. All you needed was to go one step beyond.

Ten years before the Babytime – say, in the early sixties – an adult working woman *presenting* to a doctor in ankle socks in hair-ribbons and the rest of the dressing-up and quoting children's books, would've been classifiable – a refugee from the Glass Menagerie. And quite likely to have been put away. It'd have been pathological, so to speak. Yet here was a new dress code followed, so it seemed, by half of NW1, W11 and SW3. Here a Mabel Lucie Attwell, there a clutch of sinister naughty schoolboys in flannels and little white shirts, there some Hovis lads and some street theatre clowns (Gilbert O'Sullivan and Leo Sayer had a lot to answer for . . .).

And then there were the Wendy houses. Only in the seventies could you get a wide market – wide enough to support a clutch of specialist shops and a vast freelance army of antique supermarket stall holders – selling Babystuff for home decoration. Dinkies and doggies, Mickies and Bambies, ice-cream cones and teapots on legs, first editions of the Jumblies and the Famous Five, all sold to over-twenties with a feeling for elegant design. Who sent each other Wonder-of-Woolies birthday cards, '*now you are 6*', but the Babytimers? Who played 'Goodnight children, everywhere' tapes and did old Larry the Lamb impressions? Who surrounded themselves with low-rent nostalgia? Who had the home juke-box; who became pinball wizards but the Babytimers? The Wendy house was just stuffed with archaic, winking, winsome toys; toys raised to the status of arts. The toys in the attic were well out of the closet. And who took teddy to bed?

The Babytimers were Baby-boom, and – sometimes – a bit before, kids who lived through the war or just after and often had their childhoods displaced. They weren't the face-lift generation, not yet anyway, but many were of an age to have been hippies, some even beats. They were the Pepsi generation, but they had jobs in the new straight world – a little loose at the edges – and they wanted *in*. They were weekend hippies, not streetfighting men, working in those new notionally creative industries or the soft end of the caring professions. Record companies and softback publishing, TV research and sharp-end retailing, rag trade and Arts Council, PR and women's magazines, actors and part-time antique dealers. Many were hustlers, small entrepreneurs. Many were careerists not unlike the eighties Yuppies – Young Urban Professionals. They were anything but childlike. Old rockstars – ie about 30 in the early seventies – were always Babytimers, in the van of the Babylook.

How they got that way was one of the great questions of social pathology, but Babytime – called *Playpower* – was always written into the hippie constitution. In *Playpower* Richard Neville identified three sub-groups among the new people – the counter-culture. There were the Yippies; the hairy politicals; the wretched of the earth; and the freaks, the jolly expressive counter-culturalists in street theatre and such like. Well, the freaks always had their safe Baby side, what with Yellow Submarines and the clown get-ups and white bicycles and all that. Hippie propaganda urged a childlike simplicity as political expression and the nostalgia boom uncovered its style.

### The Babytime wardrobe

Babytimers go for archaic children's clothes, usually from this century and particularly from their own childhoods – ie the forties and fifties or from the books they saw then – ie the privileged twenties and Edwardiana. They like clothes with a children's book feel – the Famous Five, *Just William* look, etc, or the winsome side of fifties Americana – Mickeymen especially. They're also very keen on the shapeless look; clothes that overpower their hapless wearers like the Jap Wrap, all those stuck-together sack things. And they're very keen on the cutesy-poo soppy end of the sportswear look too.

Some crucial items are:
- anything one-piece/unstructured, particularly bib and brace/ dungaree outfits and all adult Babygros
- hot pastels
- ankle socks – especially worn with high heels

Modern girls perform soft-shoe shuffle

- draw-string trousers (the jammies look)
- clown pants
- striped blazers
- peaked caps/urchin caps/baseball caps
- cricket clothes generally
- Rupert Bear kits
- braces for show
- silly bow-ties
- all silly knitwear including:
  bobble sweaters
  home-made sweaters
  Fairisle slipovers
- schoolboy long shorts (as per Anchor advertising)
- schoolboy macs
- knickerbockers for men
- grey flannel trousers in archaic cuts
- boys' small-pattern elastic belts
- humorous T-shirts
- rainbow scarves (street theatre)
- ra-ra skirts

When it got tough at the turn – no one looked forward to 1970 – and you were either on the bus or off it, a strange thing happened. Both the careful camp followers, who wanted back in, and the later comers, who wanted a bit of the new action, found *whimsy* the perfect antidote to Altamont *and* the straight world. To avoid *Catch 22* – back to boredom or on to real danger – you leap-frogged the whole problem. Out of the window with Peter and Tinkerbell. When you wore the new dungarees and the fun badges you were simply too young to be drafted but your uniform said, 'I'm right behind you. Workers and babies of the world unite.' In the early seventies sellers-out felt bad about it (and new recruits still saw sex'n drugs in it for them).

In Babyclothes you weren't committed, you weren't responsible. You knew Annie Hall couldn't do a proper job – a *person's* job – her jacket was too big. You were just an impulsive fun-loving spontaneous person. What's wrong with that? It was also useful professionally, for it allowed the Babies to go among the truly young and earn their living off them. Babyclothes became almost the uniform of a certain kind of disc-jockey, playgroup leader or television presenter on those Saturday morning shows.

The golden years of Babytime are over now, though there's plenty of life in it. Punks were the ultimate Babytimers; snaggled, dirty, vicious and hopeless in bondage pants and little nappies.

**Babytime footwear**

Anything soft, textile uppers in particular:
- Kickers and most other bootees
- daisy-pattern fifties sandals
- old-fashioned high heels with short socks
- black Chinese cloth slippers
- Camden Town hand-mades in hippie primaries
- bar shoes with button fastening
- plastic sandals
- most 'sneakers' (not real trainers)
- Woolies' plimsolls

**Babytime grooming**
- Raggedy Ann doll make-up (stole it from Mummy)
- hair tied up in bows in forties cutie style
- pony tails
- forties schoolboy short side-parted hair (usually reformed hippies)
- Johnson's baby shampoo and powder
- very plastic hair slides
- plastic brooches and tin or enamel badges, especially:
  early propeller planes
  ice-cream cones
  milk trucks
  Tommy the Tank Engine
  fried eggs
  palm trees
  anything Disney
  Blytonia/Noddy

gollies
teddies
'Headboy' in enamel
Vice-Headgirl
Ovalteenie or Clark's Fitting Club
'I am 9'
Scottie dogs

**Accessories**
- satchel
- music case, etc
- Mickey Mouse, etc tin lunch-box
- Mickey watches
- teddies
- big specs

Babytimers face the future: note the baseball booties and bonnet, Rupert bear trousers and big bag. Her watch features kissing couple, her earrings a red telephone box. Enjoy honey time

**Babytime décor**

Key items in the Glass Menagerie look are:
- toys in the bookcase – antique toys and children's books generally
- Dinkys
- doll collections
- teddies as décor
- Anything Mabel Lucie Attwell
- anything Blyton
- anything china on legs *à la* Strangeways
- Mickeyana (again!)
- certain Practical Styling items
- forties/fifties comic blow-ups and children's book illustrations

They screamed all day; they'd taken the call of the wild a bit far. They were *real* babies. And the punks said rude horrid things about the Baby-timers, like pointing out that they were over 18 and looked silly, and were absolutely and intracta-bly part of the great bland conspiracy – just more cynical versions of the rocking vicar syndrome.

Besides which, in 1979 came the Great Libera-tion when the Babytimers, who were doing quite nicely thank you, realised they wanted the head-mistress back, wanted the Famous Five life – with added coke – for real and didn't see why they shouldn't keep the Porsche and the cottage. They didn't have to pay lip service to the sixties ideals any more. All the old rockstars in their tracksuits and top-hat pension schemes knew it was no shame to be rich and have a jukebox collection and a garage full of big Dinkys in Victorian Berk-shire. You could dress up sometimes – and then it stuck – you could cut your hair and get a suit. You could get a bit tough and realistic. The new line of commendation – for dressing properly at 35; for eating in a *proper* restaurant; for a proper, seriously boring cocktail party was … *grown-up.*

Grown-up, just in time for last ditch procrea-tion, before the menopause. Grown-up in time for proper discipline for the children; *The Jewel in the Crown* on TV, and an entry on the Unlisted Securities Market.

But there's always New Wave.

---

- Beryl Jones work
- Manneken Pises
- toadstool lamps
- plaster dogs

### Babytime culture

From Batman on, Babytime has brought forth a string of children's entertain-ment designed solely for the over-aged. Babytimers' favourite literary refe-rences are:
- *Just William*
- Blyton
- Tin-Tin
- Asterix
- *The Little Prince*
- Rupert Bear
- Dan Dare
- 'and any fule kno *Down with Skool* is trif'

They are also very keen on:
- the Ovalteenies
- Captain Beaky
- Basil Brush (Sloanes too!)
- the Muppets
- *Yellow Submarine*
- Batman
- ET (*the Babytime film of all time*)
- *Bambi* and *Fantasia*
- R2D2
- Fritz the Cartoon Cat
- Louis Wain (Sloanes too!)
- bad fifties sci-fi movies (*le goût* Clive James)

### Babytime heroes and fellow travellers (if the baseball cap fits …)
- Peter Pan
- Frank Spencer and his lisp, Betty
- early period Elton John
- Captain Sensible
- Michael Jackson (the boy who fell to earth …)
- Anne Nightingale
- Mike Read
- ET
- John Lennon
- Diane Keaton/Annie Hall
- Terry Scott
- the late Jimmy Clitheroe
- Adrian Mole
- Bubbles Harmsworth
- Charlie Drake
- the Krankies
- Christopher Biggins

'V' wears elasticated black pumps, white socks and gym-slip-style dress in tee-shirt material

### Babytalk
- all twinkly diminutives – doggies, etc
- la di dah
- mock-pompous from early children's books
- 'they're trying to put me in a box'
- 'Blue Meanies'
- 'I'll thcream and thcream till I'm thick'
- the *Guardian's* Valentine column
- 'lashings of scrummy scoff', 'jolly japes' and everything parodied in *Five Go Mad in Dorset*, etc
- Bigglespeak – top hole, spiffing, etc
- all superlatives of wonderment

### Babyshops
- Strangeways
- Mr Freedom RIP
- Practical Styling
- Harrods children's department
- Meenys
- Milletts
- Margaret Howell
- Presents
- Parrots
- Kickers
- Nutz
- Dilemma
- Mothercare
- Woolworth's
- all joke shops

# H·O·W
# T·H·E
# W·E·D·G·E
# W·A·S
# W·O·N

Jeffrey goes Anglo

Jeffrey Daniels is P.P. Arnold! D'you know Jeffrey, the skinny one in Shalamar with the British make-over? Well Shalamar, this LA mainstream disco-group formed c. 1975, was *very* big in Britain by '82. They're black of course. They were quite popular with the British disco kids for a long while, but they really made it about the time Jeffrey had the British make-over. It looked like – well, you can see it on their earlier albums – one day Jeffrey was just your standard-make LA black-person's front-man with the wet-look hair and the major suit and wham, then he walked down the King's Road in Chelsea and got his hair conked and done in the most peculiar way – just like one of these British pop stars you see on TV and just like everyone looks in those clubs – straightened and side-parted and shaved up the back *plus pig-tails*. Well after that there was no turning back; Jeffrey said he was going to live in England, it was so exciting, all this new style. They even said the group might break up – the girl went *Anglo* too, but the other guy still seemed a bit more Stateside in his style, if you get my meaning. When Jeffrey first did *Top of the Pops*, alone with his new hair, and the new Covent Garden English clubland rig doing his mimetic body-popping, skinny legs walking on the spot – moves English kids did down English clubs – he was made. Reverse homage, for the English clubland kids had always loved American black music even though the presentation was sometimes a bit … wallyish. And here was this skinny black American getting the look as if he'd been born in Hackney.

Jeffrey is a case in point in *British Invasion*, the new game Bobby Elms and I play. In British Invasion you get five points for a good parallel with the British cultural invasion of America in the sixties and ten for a really great one. Jeffrey/P.P. Arnold is a *fifteen*. (P.P. Arnold was a very cute Ikette who rebelled when Ike and Tina were on tour here around 1965 with the Rolling Stones. She joined London clubland and made records in Britain produced by the Stones wonderboy Andrew Loog Oldham. Reverse homage again.) The rest of the picture is falling into place too. Spandau Ballet are The Who according to Bobby Elms, who's partisan because they're his friends. The Who, only better, because there are at least two *real* Faces among the Spands. Duran Duran are, we reluctantly admit, probably the Beatles. Meaning cute to teenyboppers. And Nick Heyward, ex of Haircut 100, we reckon will be Peter Noone – Herman Hermit. We have some difficulty with George – Boy George O'Dowd – however (and where does Boy Marilyn go?). You can spend hours at it, pulling up the one-hit wonders and the late-show Swinging London movies.

Anyway we've been waiting for it to happen, this British Invasion thing, since approximately 1977, me and Bobby and, oh, hundreds of other pale little British people.

There've been a lot of false starts. In 1977 and 1978 the British rock press was absolutely obsessed with the question of whether the first wave of British punk bands would make it in America. Chart action absolutely zilch *of course*, as they used to say in the music industry. Then there was the 'New Romantics' around 1981 – the Pirate Look, Adam Ant in knee breeches and suchlike. If you believed Bloomingdale's and *Interview* and Canal Street clubland were the living heart of America you might have thought England was there. But still no airplay in Iowa.

It took the visuals to do it, of course, all the promos and MTV, before young middle-America realised what these English kids *actually looked like*; that they were about half the age of the big-selling American bands (and half the age of the British groups Americans need to think mattered, who haven't mattered for *ten years*); that their hair and clothes and hence their minds were arranged in a completely different way.

Adam and George brought panto back with a bang

The biggest laugh is having Americans ask the political question; what does this *mean*, Peter? How does this all relate to the Falklands, Mrs Thatcher, the recession? As if you couldn't tell from the hair that the story is Dance Don't Riot or, as Bobby says, Anarchism through Alcoholism. The trouble is the educated American culture-vulture, who knows the names and histories of all these groups, likes to think it's all a bit deep, well, wild young rebellish or in some sense Counter-

Culturish or Alternative. Not that this is ever explicit, for these Americans know that it is somehow All Different Now, but you can tell they want something more. This middle-class love of rebel culture, of a meaning to things, means they can't see for looking. The truth is, the main political meaning is that it's politically *zero*; passive, apolitical – which is political in itself.

In fact the new culture for export is determinedly apolitical. It gets in the way of business. Look what happened with the Pistols. The thinking American confuses the Anglo style with American Avant; they are a million miles apart. The fact is British working-class kids don't really have a political vocabulary in that sense. They never did much, compared with Europeans, but now the Labour Party, the traditional party of working-class politics, is falling apart there isn't any.

Punk *was* political, but not in that way. Punk just showed what the future would be like, before conventional politicians got hold of it and tried to inject their own 1968 world-view. That was the difference between the Sex Pistols and The Clash. The Sex Pistols were *inspired, surreal* nineteenth-century guttersnipes who sang about the Queen while The Clash were really a Boho Rebel Rock Group in leather jackets with an interest in the Third World. Punk at heart was a haircut revolution not a political one. The British working class showed its mood – reactionary, passive, apathetic – when it voted for Mrs Thatcher, because she told them what to do and promised blood sweat and tears. Perry Haines, young clubland entrepreneur, stylist and so on, says 'it's more Mad Max than Mad Maggie' (Thatcher). These kids watch videos; they watch old films on TV; they look at colour magazines.

In the early and mid-sixties a most remarkable relationship started. What happened was that Britain sold young middle-America *its own black sounds.* Since the fifties when the fear of 'race music' replaced blacks with Pat Boone cover versions, American mainstream music had been steadily bled white. Black acts were for the *black market* till Motown introduced crossover. But the first British Invasion was based on kids who worshipped and copied American black acts. Look at the Beatles' and the Stones' early repertoires. They did it a million times better than most American white kids and they were race-acceptable.

But Swinging London, 'the sum total of six people's indiscretions', was otherwise a chimera, a device to sell tourism, a basis for international co-production movies financed in America and shot in London. Swinging London actually happened somewhere over the Atlantic (or in Shea Stadium). Well, they're doing it again, because the new British music that sells is dance-based. The dance comes from American blacks but it's recycled through the style machine.

The author isn't entirely innocent of America; I live part-time in the Upper East Side NY. It's a good place from which to go way Down Town by cab into wharfland, loftland, industrial wasteland, to see what's touted as the vibrant new club youth culture, the New Hip, the Video Age (ie all the descendants of Mudd Club and Danceteria, the Jim Fouratt generation). I always check it out when I'm there.

What I'm always doing when I'm down there on a visit, is checking the culture lag. It's a mean little habit, this – typical of natives of poor backward countries – of trying to find the weak comparison. With anyone from *London* in my line of work, it's the culture lag we're looking for. Thus, for instance, in late 1979, I was noticing the odd bedraggled kid done up as a Space Cadet or a Ruritanian Toy Soldier (what was sold to America in 1981 as 'New Romantic') here and there in NY hipland, and calculating when I first saw that look in London ... Autumn 1978. It's terribly consistent this culture lag, this *clothes* thing, the conclusion is basically that the Median Hip NY club person adopts the look about a year after it's broken in London clubs.

*It used to take seven hours to cross the Atlantic, but a year to put on your trousers. Before MTV that was.*

There is worse: down in NY hipland, they rarely get them right, these new London looks, because

London classic.
San Francisco
classic

their hearts aren't in it ... *into* it ... because these kids are really second-cycle hippies ... Video Bohemians. The clothes are just a look, an import speciality. They've got a lot else to think about ... a major in communication studies, an article for *Trouser Press*. The clothes are just about looking the part. Most of the New Hip in Manhattan still wouldn't get past the door in the London clubs that matter.

In London for the last twenty-five years the clothes themselves, the style, that's been the thing. It isn't symbolic, artistic, expressive of a big idea or anything *conceptual* like that (Hey man, I'm really decadent). It's all they've got and it really matters, down to the detail. And it really matters *when* you wear it. There's a tradition, a tribe of working-class stylists in London who grow up talking cut, fabric, hairdressing with a clothes culture behind them. The history was called *Mod* and the code words are sharp and neat. It takes more than a haircut and a Greenwich Village import rig-out to understand that.

*Young America* has been so out of sync with Britain over the last seven years it's fascinating – and the issue that really showed up this young divide was punk. Punk rock, which was a national convulsion in England in 1976–7, laid the ground for a whole new attitude and aesthetic. Because of punk, the streets of any large town in Britain are crawling with millennial sects of teen stylists, tribes of kids done up every which way, in every style since teen began, and all running in parallel in the most monstrous time warp you ever saw. In London now there are clubs for *rockabillies* – revivalists of *early* fifties proto-rock music and styles – and late sixties *psychedelia*, and individualists who've stolen their visuals from the eighteenth century and the twenty-first, and ten other styles and hybrids from David Bowie clones to Dizzy Gillespie lookalikes. This isn't Bohemia, this obsession with style, it's *national*, it isn't, say, cable TV, it's *network*.

It was a mark of America's isolation in the seventies that a kind of Swinging London Mark II was conceived – and has almost gone – with minimal attention from mainstream American media

kids' race memory is the Wedge: I don't think I've ever seen the Wedge in America – not even on a flaming faggot, as they say. It's parted to one side – or a straight flop over the eyes like Bryan Ferry – swept to the back, almost like a DA and carved short on the neck. The original, done by Trevor Sorbie in 1974, hasn't had the credit it deserves, this flying wedge of straight blond androgyne hair. When they first cut it and blow it dry they keep on brushing the sides flat, pushing them back underneath the long bits at the crown so the bob part of it is resting on the pushed-back horizontal part. The stylists' trick then is to *let it go*, so it springs out, the long bits bouncing out on top of the side, all that bouncing volume disappearing into razored flatness with nothing hippy or impromptu around the neck. Bare necks, visible ears, with bouncing subversive hair on top. What could be more irritating than this long-short combination? It makes punk spikes look obvious. Did Trevor, 'creative director' at Vidal Sassoon then, know what style meant, where all this layering would lead? The Wedge is the most influential hairstyle of the decade, and decades run from fives to fives, 1975 to 1985, you see.

In the original, which was *very* stylised, the underneath was coloured darker to emphasise the shape in the Vidal Sassoon tradition. In the original, the Wedge was for girls. Well, if the girls have it, there's no stopping the boys. And the boys wore it down the clubs where other boys, straight but loose, picked up on it and, by 1975–6, it was the uniform for the southern English, club-going, working-class soul stylist who is the hero of our story.

Ah, did your ears prick up at that, middle-class thinkers? Working-class! Did a vision of working-class traditions, of blue-collar heroics, Neanderthal punks, or even ... *Bruce Springsteen*, posed against *wrecked cars* or something funky and devastated, flash on? Well, no ... at this point you should be thinking of David Bowie. Bourgeois

or ordinary young Americans. The fact was that from 1976 on, British working-class youth ran the pilot programme for the 1980s. But, out of context, reflected occasionally in freak-show snippets on American TV, the new British styles just came over as a series of separate merchandising hypes: New Looks for Seventh Avenue.

The one that really caught the American eye two years ago was 'New Romantic'. People I talked to in New York seemed to think it'd come out of nowhere, a bit of fun, like a new movie outdating last year's big thing. They'd bought the idea of a lot of kids done up like old movie stills. They thought these kids represented a reaction against the noisy, violent, nihilistic, underclass punks they'd been hearing about. Well, not only was this untrue but, by the time it came out, it was out of date as well: the truth was *it was the same people all along*. The first punks *were* the New Romantics, but before anything those working-class stylists were *soulboys*.

If you want to understand the London attitude, to penetrate to the very heart of the ideology, the differences between London and New York Hip and What Really Matters in Life, we have to look at *hairdressing*. The key hair-style in the London

Bohos have the *strangest* idea of working class. *Rock*, says Gary Kemp of Spandau Ballet, is the middle-class vision of the working class.

And, when you think uniform, picture it roughly like this: say, a big sweatshirt from a snob Italian maker, so snob there's no words, but based on grey with horizontal stripes in something subtle, dusty pink, say (wear an American university one and you're dead), and the Fiorucci pegs, the one classic thing they ever did, Fiorucci, one good reason the kids would make the trip, say twenty miles from Hornchurch – to Knightsbridge SW1 where they buy the Look, or South Molton Street where a shop called Browns sells *Calvin* and *Ralph* and *Giorgio Armani* at couturier mark-ups.

The social geography of London hip is different. The club kids have always gone uptown 'Up West' to Mayfair W1, Knightsbridge SW1, and King's Road SW3. Manhattan's punks may have gone downtown to the Bowery, but the stylists don't truck with *slumming*. The Fiorucci pegs aren't Western, or fifties stovepipe mock-prole macho, the way they bell slightly at the hips, the way the bottom seams are sewn in so it's kind of gathered and, of course, so you can see the socks. It's ambiguous, almost effeminate. This isn't Frye Boot country, besides which the Fiorucci pegs are made from a different, lighter kind of denim so they hang differently. More drape, you see. There are two inches of sock on the instep, white or cream wide ribs, before you get to the tab on the pumps. *Loafers.* Imagine some Italian at work on your Weejuns, soft leather instead of cardboard with a close edge sole instead of mudguards. This white socks and pumps combo is fine with a variety of important footwear, including the plain dancing master pump or even – what London black kids are doing now – shiny patent evening shoes with grosgrain bows. Try wearing *that* down the PTA!

The black boys who are doing this grosgrain evening slipper thing are also wearing full tilt barathea evening dress combos with narrow bowties. It's this kind of boy, you see, who is the soul brother, get-on-down, state second colour choice, and best mate of the white club kids. These boys either have the wet-look, high yeller curls, like Michael Jackson, or the shaped shaved crop like David Clay, this British black athlete who became a model. By now you will have formed a definite impression. You'd be wrong. These boys are straight, most of them.

*Jean-Pierre's Club* is about eight foot square. No, allow for exaggeration, twenty by thirty absolute maximum. Studio it ain't: like many others of the kind, it serves a mix of tourists. Latins who work in catering here in Soho, London West One, and junior typists. Jean-Pierre, who's as Cockney as they come, used to be bar manager at Le Beat Route, and he's put £80,000 into this place. He's got plans for it. He's already put in a pro disco lighting system – blue, red, white: blue, red, white – and he's got plans for the upstairs restaurant which, at the moment, is buttoned red, vinyl banquettes round formica tables in two rows to the door, with rough-cast Spanish lights above. Very basic really.

Jean-Pierre, who's 32, wants to attract *the class trade*. He's explaining it to Bobby Elms – how he'll strip out the banquettes, and replace them with the kind of stuff the High Spenders like: sueded wallpaper, carpet, maybe cane and rattan. He doesn't want Bobby to get going until then. He doesn't really want Bobby bringing his friends down until he's done the make-over. Bobby really likes Jean-Pierre, but at 22 he's got a lot more experience of the great world and doesn't know quite how to tell J-P that *he's got it all wrong.* The disco lights mean fuck all, the vinyl banquettes are fine – in fact his friends will like them – all they need is somewhere to make breakfast after the all-nighters.

Bobby's done very well out of the Scene. As the token Cockney clubland kid, he's media perfection. Bobby will rattle on for hours about the Scene, about trousers and haircuts, working-class young London and creative vitality, so that Jean-Pierre's modest boîte ('My mother was a French woman from the upper class but my dad was a Cockney. He never felt at ease in all that.') could, one suspects, easily turn up in a bemused journalist's copy as Swinging London Mark II. Bobby's job to date has been Minister of Information for the Scene, now, which was dimly perceived in America as 'Spandau Ballet play the Underground Club, New York', hosted by Jim Fouratt. (Jim was bringing the Scene in as a Manhattan Import Speciality.) That was what it was all about until MTV.

The Scene is Bob's story and it's earned him two years on the rock papers with a lot of good dinners in smart restaurants from record companies and journalists and TV people just cottoning on. Bob's been joint presenter on a TV 'youth' show – not peak-time but network, a start. He's doing new music news for a US radio network. Now he wants to do something a bit entrepreneurial, which is to take over Jean-Pierre's little place for one special night a week. The deal is this – Bob has the club for a night, pays for the door, does the publicity, brings the crowd, and gives Jean-Pierre a guaranteed take. That's the way the Scene is actually arranged, for the last couple of years anyway. It's not really where, it's who's on the door. The portable club works like a rent party or a black 'blues': go down these places when the crowd's gone and there's nothing there. *It's all about who's on the door.*

It dates back to 1978 and Billy's. There's nothing there at Billy's now, which is just mythology, but Billy's was really the start of the new portable clubland. How Billy's started, roughly, goes like this. In 1978, after the first London punk scene fell apart, the various constituent parts went back to first base, which were ... David Bowie, Bryan Ferry, soul music and Posing for the Haircut Kids who wore the Wedge, and back to the roots socialism, rock and roll populism and other forms of alien behaviour for latecomers.

The style punks went down the popular gay clubs, which was no big deal in London – if you're thinking Village People or Anvil/Mineshaft/Toilet horror stories, forget it; that wasn't the style in London, things are more relaxed. They let in straights, they let in girls. Billy's was this little nothing gay club in Meard Street, a Dickensian cross street in Soho with girls in the windows and 'French Model, First Floor' on the bell pushes. And Maltese boys in Travolta suits down at street level – Olde Tyme Soho. Billy's was another little box club until Bobby's friends, Steve and Rusty Egan, changed it all. Steve and Rusty took over Billy's on Tuesdays, when Rusty was DJ and Steve was on the door and they played *Futurist*, as it came to be called.

They played Bowie and Bryan, and a lot of this curious German band, Kraftwerk, who produced a kind of smart disco-muzak which was all synthesizer, all techno. They didn't even appear themselves. Dummies stood in for them. That was all the thing in late '78. Stylisation, cool, distance, *posing*. It's all changed now.

And, how to explain Billy's: Billy's was totally interchangeable with Jean-Pierre's place, i.e. another thirty by twenty basement, like they all are. It's like the Cariba which is Uptown Spade; or

*Blitz: we can be heroes for ever and ever*

Spats; or Crackers – you only know where you are by who's there and what they're playing. *These places aren't heavy on décor.* They don't go in for squalour, either. The haircut stylists don't want the Mark I Canal Street Mudd Club look. The industrial shed, the punk lavatories, don't appeal. That's for *students*, bourgeois. It's SoHo not Soho. In Billy's, winter 1978, they didn't *need* décor, the space captains, the Ruritanian toy soldiers in uniforms and sashes and little caps, heavy make-up all round, and great big pantomime Turkish trousers like Bowie wore on tour that year. The Billy's look was a long way beyond basic stylists, more evolved. The kids at Billy's were on their way to becoming art objects, but certain parts of the traditional story persisted, like an enduring affection for David Bowie and soul music. It was at Billy's that the white-socks working-class stylists first started to meet the white faces, the art students and professional visuals from St Martin's and the Royal College of Art, who started playing back at them that they were living The Life.

Anyway, that's the history of London's new clubland now. No multi-million-dollar aircraft hangar discos like Bonds on Times Square. No Liz and Liza, precious little coke, *everyone a star.*

Billy's, autumn 1978: Steve and Rusty reintroduce posing with the Ruritanian Toy-Soldier look

The kids, it goes without saying, dance well. And to dance well you need soul music. There's always an overlay on it, of course, a fashion thing; anything from Peggy Lee to Frank Sinatra to Africana, but for basics you need black dancing music. Like who? Like it doesn't matter, like this is serviceable music, it works or it doesn't, and you want the newest on twelve inches from America and, of course, James Brown and Sly were great but you're not going to get yourself into a sweat about *history* or what a funk act thinks about the world, because – and here is the point – it's just like getting supplies, not a great 'musical' thing.

*Mighty, mighty, spade and whitey.* In the hardcore soulie's clubs Up West and in the London hinterland, black and white kids *always* mixed *for the Life*. That comes a long way ahead of the sex combos – it isn't black boys and white girls – and it isn't slumming, because these white kids are from the same backgrounds as the black ones, the same streets, the same schools, *soul brothers*, so to speak. *Nowhere in the world is black American dancing music more cherished than in England*. Since Frankie Lymon and the Teenagers in 1956, since Motown started filtering over here in 1962, there's been this white working-class soulie tradition, bigger, more rooted than anything you ever heard about Swinging London.

The first stylist rule goes: when you see the wrong people doing it, you move on.

When New Romantic went national, was on English TV and the *national* papers, the originals simply disappeared, the first portable clubs folded their tents, the kids went for another number in the cupboard – something subtler – and musically they went back to their roots. Those outfits weren't a statement, didn't say how the kids felt about Life or any big stuff. It's *dressing up* that's the statement, caring about clothes, that's the thing, knowing the details, doing it *first* that matters. Plastic sandals; peg pants; haircuts; evening slippers; TIMING; precision; collars; button-downs; tabs; TIMING; *finesse*. Sharp, the national culture of *sharp dressing* – from Mods in sharp shiny mohair with knife-edge creases, subtly subversive, to soul boy, more relaxed, more casual ... Casual that

takes two hours to put on. (The white Lacoste-type sportshirt over the Fioruccis with the electric-blue Benetton sweater with the arms linked around the neck, *sportif*.) Casual that's squeaky clean. Casual that hates hippies, rockers, and lowlife. Sharp dressing.

After the sixties, America never had *sharp* dressing as part of the national teen story – not for ordinary, suburban, blue-collar kids anyway. Caring like these little English fashion intellectuals was for ethnics, fags, and other cheesy outsiders. Real American life was too casual. But in Britain there was always an underground dialogue for lapels, haircuts, going Up West, the blue-collar suburban, black and white kids buying in the sharpest shops in the best shopping district. They don't go to those ethnically favoured downtown ghetto polyester-look bridge and tunnel type Travolta dumps (London kids laughed themselves sick at the Travolta character's dumb get-up in *Saturday Night Fever* and his two years out headband and hopeless dance routines in *Staying Alive*).

These kids have been sharp and neat since the first boxy Italian suits came over in the late fifties and their fathers and big brothers went suddenly ... *modernist* in Perry Como haircuts and quiet knit shirts. That was the reaction to the Rebel Rocker look – the Neanderthal 'Teddy Boy' style of the mid-fifties, the first British teenagers ever.

Why do these kids put it all into looks, looks, looks – so much energy and cleverness going into clothes and clubs and dance-floor stardom? *What else is there* – there was never a young working-class politics in Britain, like in Europe; middle-class American summer-campish open-air athletics and body culture; no sun so no silver surfers or street life; not that much leisurely sex – they did better with their clothes on.

And here was never much education (only 25 per cent of English kids go to college). Now, like the punks said, there's No Future. For most American middle-class kids it's still a little *conceptual*, remote, this 'No Future' business, which is tied up with the Sex Pistols and other kinda weird stuff from England. While they're still studying for the video arts major, or just trying harder to get into IBM, it's more about how things aren't that great – rather than No Jobs, No Expectations, no nothing very much.

In England, it's all turned in on clothes and dancing. These kids are *like black Americans* up to a point. But they don't stay in their ghettos, they come Up West, *above their station* to the same places where Tom Wolfe found The Life in 1965, in the West End, round Soho (and, yes, round Carnaby Street, though only tourists shop there and only Asians trade there now) because that's where those little clubs were and always will be – the home of the dancing tribes from the early Mods to the first Soulies who loved Tamla Motown and Otis Redding, Wilson Pickett and other fantastically more obscure imports.

In urban England from 1958 to 1981 the real white Negro wasn't a wistful middle-class (Jewish) college kid who wished he were a ghetto black (a junkie, a hipster, a jazzman, a pimp, any of the *picturesque* stuff, all strength and pathos) but a sharp-faced, sharp-dressed white working-class kid who simply *knew* the black kids and liked the same music, the clothes and dancing. These kids aren't wistful, they're in there, blacks aren't *Another Country*, they're *next door*.

The Geno story's at the heart of it: Geno Washington, a secondary American black soul singer, ex-GI, had a residence in the Brixton Ram Jam Club in working-class south London in the mid-sixties. Geno was soul legend afterwards. Those sharp-dressed, whey-faced undersized Mods loved this shiny black man with the tearing rhythmic brass which suited their tight rhythmic dancing; the back-of-the-heel work, spins and chops. In the photographs – which, weirdly, like all pre-1967 London Mod photographs, look totally Now – they're looking at Geno like a football hero, like he's won something for them. And in 1980 a band called Dexy's Midnight Runners – a name like that means starting from myth – got to No. 1 with a brassy new White Soul number 'Oh Geno' – the most heart-tearing bit of music intensity that year. It's about the Heritage, and Speed, and Soul, and Spade and Whitey and foaming amphetamine prole kids staying up all night in Central London anytime at all from 1961 on.

So when the 'Mod' period officially ended, in 1966–7, according to bourgeois media folk who were mad for Psychedelia and West Coast Underground Wonders like the Grateful Dead on Import, it simply went on underground. Out of the media spotlight, Soul was treasured, rallied to in underground conventions. Throughout the seventies coachloads of kids from over the country made the pilgrimage north to Wigan, the *greyest* nineteenth-century Lancashire industrial town, for the Wigan Casino Soul all-nighters, dancing for ten hours solid (you travel with your clothes on hangers to avoid the creasing). In the lobbies they sold and exchanged rare twelve-inchers, new US imports by Phillydogs you've never heard of, and special cuts from Stax and Atlantic and pure Collector's Corner madness. On the floor they kept it going because they *danced themselves dizzy* with back-flips and athletics.

And so did the Boys, because in Boystown they *needed* the clubs and hated Woodstock and all the hideous student stuff. The gay clubs, which were more little Soho boxes thirty by twenty, indistinguishable from the kids' clubs, kept the black dancing music going. They had a different brand (at Christmas the boys would dress as the Supremes and mime to the Motown Golden Greats).

A roll-call of the people who went down the clubs for the music, the clothes, the sex, the stardom would be a roll-call of the Modern Movement … *all* the First Punks (Johnny Rotten and Siouxsie) and those 'New Romantics' … Steve Strange, the one you've seen in America with the Gaucho outfits and all, and his clever business partner Rusty Egan, the people who started Billy's. The whole explosive fragmenting mass of eighties British style has actually come out of these tight little boxes. The American Hip, by contrast, stands for *hippy* … with a haircut.

The American backbeat was always 'rock'; slack-gutted men with long hair doing guitar solos. And the American alternative was wretched art ghettos like SoHo NY where you could have fun guying the fifties and sixties with video and hyper-realism. White America never learnt about *posing*.

To be fair, America never had Bowie and Bryan Ferry, who between them in the early seventies set the whole thing up for punk and Romantic, for stylists and Indoor Men. Bryan? I once went to a dinner-party for some LA movie producers. The girl who gave it is *the* London model agent and *definitive* and, of course, to add colour she'd asked Bryan.

I talked to these LA hitmen in the corner about units and grosses and those *music industry* things and they asked about here and I tried to explain there was kind of a Glam Revival and how it's like Bryan – him over there, Bryan Ferry – *and they didn't know who Bryan Ferry was.*

Understanding London pose practically begins with a working knowledge of Bryan Ferry's outfits gathered in your teens – Rocker Surreal in 1972, Tuxedo Hollywood in 1973, GI in 1974, Roman Spiv in 1975. The girls on his covers were as exaggeratedly peachy red-lipped, stiletto-heeled dream women as you could get. Kari-Ann, Amanda Lear, Jerry Hall. His band, Roxy Music, gave shows like fashion shows, their visuals set the style for the next six months. Instead of despising fashion, like the *rock* people, they were part of it, like Grace Jones. Club kids, soul boys, faggots, fashion people *loved* the pastiche, the posing. Bryan Ferry didn't sell in America.

To the kids Bowie was ... the best haircut of 1972 (spiky on top, longer at the back) and of '75 when David wore the Wedge and *plastic sandals* in *The Man Who Fell to Earth*. These plastic sandals were fundamental – kids' bathing sandals in tinted clear jellyfish plastic in unspeakable Day-Glo colours, worn with peg pants and a feel for elegance. Quite a leap for working-class kids who never used to wear anything too ... tasteless, kitschy. It could've been embarrassing but David made it all right. David Bowie had this extraordinary effect in Britain right from the early seventies, of producing more *clones* than anyone else. His fans didn't just want to look like him, though that was vital, but to *be* like him completely. Bowie

*David made it all right*

opened up the world for the uptight working-class stylist because he was a sharp dresser, so the big idea he was putting across slipped down easily. What Bowie was actually saying to the kids was art: you can be an art object.

Bryan Ferry was art too, because nothing he did was entirely what it seemed, there was always cleverness and detachment and taste in it. Between them they were more subversive than a boatful of chemicals. They gave the stylists ideas, made them self-conscious. And they were credible because they looked good, which was the real acid test. They understood posing, they knew the music was just the soundtrack to the Life and their shows were Shows. They were star stylists, not musicians.

Musicians simply didn't mean a thing down the clubs. Bryan and David were the only white stars they identified with. As Bryan and David played identity games through the seventies with new personalities and periods, just like real artists, things got a bit more fantastic down there, more ambiguous, time-warpy, cross-gender and generally strange because the kids were starting to play about with all the old symbols of the teen cultures and jumble them up. They were buying second-hand; raiding the past, art directing whole clubland set-pieces of their own.

To be precise, in 1975 a soul freaks' club called the Goldmine on Canvey Island, an ugly mole of Essex coastland populated by refugees from London's working-class East End, was in the up-

The father of them all, Bowie, in 1975. Cf Simon Taylor of Duran Duran

market *Sunday Times* colour supplement because the kids in there, so the paper said, were dressing up and dancing to *Glenn Miller*. And the writers were asking if this meant a revival in forties Swing and other utterly daft missed-the-point questions like that, as if the kids had signed up for some Daddies 'Classics of Swing' Archive Society. The music wasn't the point at all; the dressing up, the staging's the point. By the time the picture was out they were on to another look. And between times they were back to Earth Wind and Fire, Kool and the Ohio Players. Basic black dancing music.

Just once what was actually happening Down There showed up, nearly five years before the national press discovered the New Romantics,

and six years before America saw *anything*.

New Romantics was a marvellously cynical name, wonderfully memorable and inappropriate for a group of little stylists who filled in the blank in the most literal way possible. Kids who'd gone out of the twentieth century, who seemed to see history – and the old movies – as one great dressing-up chest. It's so easy in Britain, all the old costume drama material's so accessible – royalty, the courts – all those knee-breeches on video.

It was building for years, the stylists scene, down the clubs, until punk. Punk was style too and a lot of the stylists were involved. But punk was so intense it knocked people off course, left them confused. The stylists didn't really regroup properly till 1978, and when they did their *vocabulary* was wider, with more ideas, more discordant strange things. They'd seen the punks explode twenty-five years of youth culture and teenage mythology just by showing kids how to do it for themselves – heroes were redundant, stars were redundant, rebels were redundant. And *rock* was certainly over.

Shell-shocked stylists naturally took to *Futurism* fashion-show music: music to pose to, seamless and soothing, restating the eternal values, haircuts and trousers.

It didn't last; down the club they always got back to dancing. People who'd never actually been down the London clubs took this idea of *posing* they'd read about very literally of course – when the New Romantic style spread to provincials who didn't really have the stylist roots, you'd see kids done up like the crowd scene in the school play just *standing around*, waiting to be recognised, not knowing that real infantas, true mad monks would dance themselves dizzy. When New Romantic went public the kids went into Fake Funk, and Mock Salsa – Dancing Music was the word. By then, the temporary club idea had taken over the city's basements.

Business was desperate in 1980 and clubmen listened to any kid who'd walk in and promise a guaranteed take for the night. In two years a new scene developed which was . . . ten scenes, twenty scenes, you could go through twenty-five years in a week like some great multi-tracking video, or a lot of last 'Late Late Shows'. And 'pop' – the English sixties idea of mass popular music for tinies – went through an astonishing revival based almost entirely on *visuals*. To the world English art now is the pop promo video, it's the golden age of the promo video.

London is the world capital of pictures-to-music, pictures selling music, network TV shows presenting nineteen-year-old stylists to nine-year-olds, all the stuff that was cooking up down the clubs three years ago, pumped straight out in the TV networks in this tight little island. Every week *millions* of kids watch the Everyday Surreal on video promos on *Top of the Pops* – the English network TV pop show – and take in more advanced tuition in Avant Styling than in a year of Manhattan Cable TV's freak hours. The abiding image of eighties Britain is still Adam Ant – 1981 No.1 record seller – in eighteenth-century costume and make-up wearing a Sony Walkman in a promo video designed for the under-twelves.

Crisis Britain has more video machines, more home computers, per head than any other Western country – the US included. Recession Britain sinks beneath the economic slime *absolutely wired*.

*Left* The Goldmine, Canvey Island, 1975: fastidious style-obsessed black and white Essex overflow heroes in at the beginning

Spandau at the beginning, November 1980

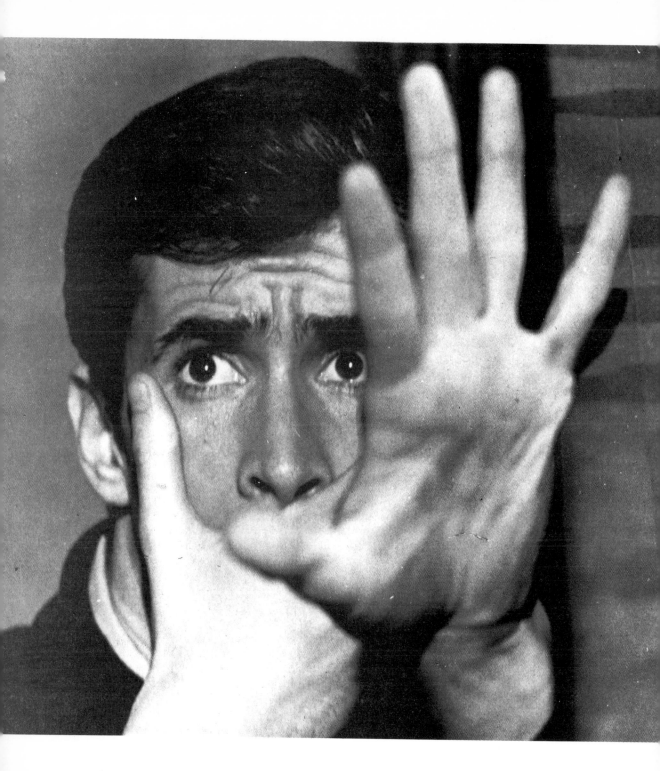

WORLDS APART

A classic Nutty Boy pose: cf the cover of Bowie's 'Heroes' album
which sadly we are not permitted to reproduce by order of the
Bowie Foundation

## C·L·U·B·T·I·M·E

# N·E·U·R·O·T·I·C  B·O·Y
# O·U·T·S·I·D·E·R·S

Group styles aren't always about belonging. There's one with a respectable two-hundred-year tradition about *not belonging*. Our heroes here are the Neurotic Boy Outsiders, and the battle to be different. *You're not alone*, turn on with me.

The first Neurotic Boy Outsider was the eighteenth-century teen-poet Chatterton. The Victorians saw Chatterton as a kind of posthumous pop star because he was arty and sensitive and he topped himself at an early age. They felt he was like the nineteenth-century Romantic poets. Now, viewed from a distance, those lads – otherwise very dissimilar, they didn't think much of each other – had certain things in common. They stood outside *comfortable society*. They were off the rails. They were obsessive, turbulent souls.

The Romantic poets all had interesting problems. Byron had a club foot, related to women rather badly, and wanted to fight for freedom. Keats was small, common and consumptive. They worried about the problems of the world – especially Shelley. You see, they had A Concept. They were individuals. They had *images*.

A bit later, well quite a lot later really, in 1942,

this Frenchman called Camus put the word to it and actually wrote a book called *The Outsider*. Now, French intellectuals are a bit strong for Anglo-Saxon taste and Camus was knocking on a bit then, and he was a serious man in a serious time. But nonetheless the word, and the image, caught on.

The pattern was established. NBOs all had problems, because they were rather artistic, talented types. People didn't understand them sometimes because they couldn't always *explain* how they felt, not in prose anyway. It was too intense. This meant they became very touchy and gestury. NBOs had to show how they felt by what they wore. This meant they went in for a lot of black, because it showed that they were moody, and deep.

The first mass *popular* NBOs turned up in the post-war movies. James Dean had a lot of NBO style – off-screen and on. But his great coup in the NBO stakes was dying. That was always a good NBO career move. He didn't get old. Or fat; Marlon Brando had some of the inarticulateness, but he was too fat. The post-war convention echoed the

Romantic one – NBOs must be thin. If consumption was out – a drug problem was the answer. But the man who *made* the style, and who, on screen, took the biscuit for multiple problems, was Anthony Perkins. He was amazingly thin, perpetually moody and he had everything going for him. Like the best fifties NBOs, he was typecast as a *psychopath*. This was a new word for someone who kills people because he finds them hard to relate to. He made the Neurotic Boy Outsider part of the American dream.

England never really got psycho-neuro boys right in the films. But they started trying in pop. Adam Faith *looked* right for the bed-sit market. He was little and thin and his hair came forward in a thinking man's Polish actor Hamlet fringe and he wore black sometimes. But he was a bit *chirpy*, and his songs were, well, distinctly undeep.

In the sixties Pete Townshend was promising.

His first songs had all the NBO themes. He was obviously a big worrier – about the world, about his looks, about practically everything. He was all heart. But it was difficult to be a credible outsider on those lines with Moon and Daltrey around. Moral: NBOs are *loners*.

Then someone came along who got the style *exactly* right – Scott Walker. Scott Walker was a bit of a heart-throb in the sixties. One third of the Walker Brothers at first. He achieved true Arty Neuro status when they broke up and he could sing deep songs by Frenchmen on his own. He also did a lot for *shades* as a moody device. Shades were the Sony headphones of their day. He wore his shades perpetually, and he was *very* thin. It goes without saying that he was often found in extremely low moods wandering around and worrying about something too big to explain.

But hold on, can't you hear how *David's* suffering? This thin white duke was the original ET. And boy, was he sensitive, he couldn't even bear his own company for long. The cover of Bowie's

'Heroes' sums it all up. The Absolute Torture of being that kind of person. It's really all too much. There it is in black and white and David's in Berlin rather than cosy old Beckenham and he obviously knows what the future's going to be like. It's *complete* misery.

After this worried boy fell to earth lots more lads positively rained down. By the late seventies everybody seemed to have read the NBO handbook. And you couldn't move for lonely, anguished young men with synthesisers and pancake make-up. They had the most amazing worries and the most obscure references. That was at the same time as the New Romantics, as people called them, to whom the nation's window-dressers owed a huge debt. Let no one say they've had no influence. And those boys weren't just posey, they actually said that *the pose was the thing*, the art, so to speak. They said that you

didn't actually have to suffer, that you didn't have to be a poet. You could live by night in black and white.

Despite this heresy the young intellectual person's bible, the *New Musical Express*, continued to chart the problems of people like David Sylvian of Japan and the late Ian Curtis of Joy Division. Joy Division were probably the last of the genuine article; but the NBO *style* soldiered on with all sorts of pale faces and black clothes. There was even a band called Southern Death Cult, who were on the thin side. By now all this had turned the people who didn't want to belong into one of the biggest singles clubs in the world. They were all fully paid-up members. No one forced them to join. Does this mean that Neurotic Boy Outsiders are *dying out*, I hear you ask? On the contrary: everyone can join the Outsiders' club now. It's only fair.

# T·E·L·E·V·I·S·I·O·N
# F·A·M·I·L·I·E·S

**September 1982**

You don't know with a man like Ted Turner . . . he might not know who one was or, strictly speaking, had been. This cornball-homily, JR-style, Atlanta cable-television millionaire might not know the last British Ambassador to Washington, the chairman of TV-am and once one of the cleverest young men in England. One has to allow for that. The slight social strain of this utterly ridiculous unworthy thought does something to Peter Jay's rubbery *jolie-laide* mask. (A girl has said to me that 'He looks like he's melting – in a very sexy way.' The Beast of Ealing Common.) Actually, the ex-ambassador is a very big man, as Ted Turner is a very big man, and they look at each other, these big champions, and Jay says, 'I'm Peter Jay. I gave the lecture last year and I-was-very-interested-in-what-you-said-about . . .'

Ted Turner does grade I greetering but his eyes don't move too much, suggesting to Jay, Wykehamist ex-ambassador, son of Wykehamist Labour minister, and really quite well-dressed in light-weight Prince of Wales check suit with one little darn on the shoulder and a faded coral crêpe-de-Chine tie, that his suspicion was very probably right. *Ted doesn't know*.

Now the Jays are a scrumptious family, what with Peter and Douglas and the heavenly Chelsea-comes-to-the-liberal-intelligentsia Jay Twins, Sussex University's mid-sixties answer to Shrimpton and Patti Boyd and everyone, The Look on campus. They could have gone to Oxbridge, but they were pioneer plate-glass. And the girls worked in TV for a while as researchers, whipping their straight blonde hair up and down the corridors at BBC Television Centre. TV has some more obvious dynasties – plutos like the Grades or the Bernsteins; even the Crawleys had two generations going – but if you wanted to pick a symbol of the nicest type of television family, *the type the people who worked in TV wanted to be like*, you couldn't do better than the Jays. Even the

WORLDS APART

*Above* Ted Turner in an out-take from his mini-series 'Atlanta'

*Left* Delicious, clever, thoughtful, Kennington-man style, ex-ambassador Peter Jay confronts the message in the medium

now-separated Mrs Jay (Sunny Jim's daughter, famous now through Nora Ephron) is a BBC worker.

Peter Jay's 1981 McTaggart Lecture at the Edinburgh Television Festival reads to have been very different from Ted's. Jay had created a thoughtful scenario of future television, with cables and satellites all throwing the stuff at us as one walked through free air like a TV market. The *regulatory* nanny figures, he said, were only endorsing monolithic or '*duo/oligo-lithic*' franchises. They wanted to keep control. But deregulation was clearly right, went on the one-time Economics Editor of *The Times*.

In his talk Peter Jay posed, of course, a number of *perceptive questions* and ended with some suggestions for 'shape and standards'. Bou-oum ... Any literary person would have known at once that it was just the sound the old woman hears in the Indian cave in *Passage to India*. Bou-oum. Utterly dull.

Ted Turner's style is a bit different; well, a whole lot different. Ted, for a start, talks to these upper serious television families, the Brightest and the Best of Hampstead, Islington, Barnes, Richmond, Oxbridge roughly 1952-1965 ... well, he talks to them as to the Atlanta Chamber of Commerce; *as a collection of good old boys*.

Now the audience is well into double-tracking at these tones, but after the first couple of sentences – no snickering there – they have decided to relish Ted for the great sly *character* actor he is. Only a man who'd made – what, $12 million or is it $120 million – all that, from cable, could talk so down-homey. Here is JR – but he probably went to Harvard Business School. Here is Ted saying of cable proliferation some version of 'Hell, ah reckon two is better than one, and three is better than two ...' And that it's pretty easy to build up a TV station; anyone can do it. Ted is a straight go-for-growth man. Oh, the simplicity of great men. *Truly deregulated.*

But as it goes on, this particular episode – pan to Sue Ellen's ashen face, move across the rows of puzzled television families – something seems to have gone wrong, something frankly embarrassing

has happened. After going about five minutes it seems that Ted is simply *going to go on like this to the end.* Instead of switching into the language of *addressing the issues and thinking it through* and all that. For this audience, this is like not having your brain on straight.

The greatest shock is that Ted seems determined, mid-speech, to offer up some Coca-Cola style universal kitsch sentiments and to say a bad word for the bomb. They would far rather hear – well, anything JR-ish – than this. Everyone had been struck by this bold choice of speaker, but this lecture was just better forgotten. He simply *hasn't* addressed the issues. Let's have Humphrey Burton next year.

In the bar of the George, temporary centre of the TV festival where you get television family members at the level of Melvyn Bragg, chairman of the festival, and Aubrey Singer, (ex-) MD BBC Television and suchlike, all swirling around the antiqued chesterfield double-backed sofas in front of the new carved pine fireplace underneath the tartan hangings right there in the middle of grey Georgian Edinburgh, our temporary TV village. There's Paul Callan of the *Daily Mirror* talking to Ugly George about how he gets women to strip for him. George is a cable-TV person, once a pretty college professor, now getting paunchy, jowly and spoilt-looking, who's got a show on Manhattan cable TV which is all about that. Take it off and get on TV. Like an early seventies rock star, George has a sort of silver-paper romper suit with a *sexy* T-shirt and a Dory Previn fruzzle. George carries his cameras on his back. George is his own crew, his own media package. George is a specialist and, to use a term that's very buzzy this year, a narrowcaster (the other one is 'ghetto', which is a different way of looking at narrowcasting).

This is one of many such interviews George gives during the festival. Arguably, George has more column inches, more air time, than any other single contributor, for his *refreshingly simple* philosophy, his *engagingly frank* view of his responsibility to his audience. Anyway, he's the only contributor who's dressed up specially. George tells me he feels the TV situation is getting

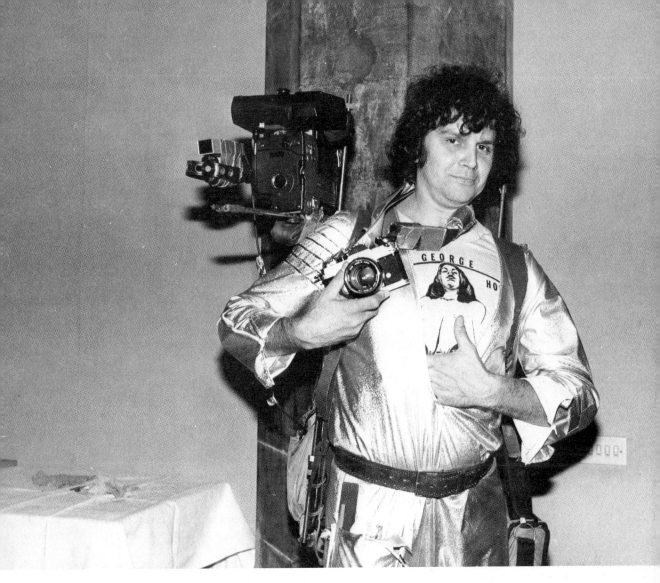

Dirty George makes
his pitch in babystyle
silver romper suit

more interesting in Britain now and there could be
opportunities for his package. That's why he's
here.

Well, Ted is a fascinating man and George is fun
for the populars but really a distraction – so let's
get on to the really important stuff like the Falklands Coverage debate (freedom of the press ...
sorry, airways – many of these people have done
time in Fleet Street) and the Politics of Change
('How the revolution in communications might
affect the political process') and STV's party in the

Radical Alan Yentob of 'Arena' makes a forceful point. Television families take it

Dynamic dynastic Michael Grade knows the bottom line. Television families remain unconvinced

'The Generation Game's' corduroy-jacketed likely lad Melvyn Bragg can take a joke

Scottish Parliament building and Granada's in the Signet Library. But there is no avoiding it: *Ted and George are the spectres at the feast for the television families.* Since the liberal hour of television – roughly 1967, when the Frost-fronted consortium got the rich London Weekend franchise from the sludgy Rediffusion on the promise of the New Stuff – the TV contractors have been full, at their middle and senior operating levels, with a special kind of person. Consider, for instance, a caricature: Christopher X, 41 – pallid, skinny good looks, lean legs in faded cords, grey shoes with little punched dots. Creative. Knitwear and a fishing bag – a first in PPE from Keble, lives in Islington, head of current affairs at XTV, won his spurs for his coverage of the Rhodesia crisis and an early-seventies documentary series on the poverty trap called *Casualties.* His second wife, Lucy, is a freelance journalist specialising in home affairs and women's issues. There you have it. Once, the *TV producer strike rate* was significant in determining the character and potential of a housing area. These new people were recruited by the TV contractors as they grew – and grew richer – with scarcely a hitch through the sixties and seventies until 1979. The older TV types – bitsas from Brit show biz, *characters*, BBC radio men, were dying off by the mid-sixties and the Outsiders contractors looking for Establishment cred and access bought the cleverest graduates – with a heavy Oxbridge emphasis. Throughout that period, television was the number-one student career-choice.

While the commercial TV contractors were up-marketing their ranks like crazy, the BBC was loosening up, and the ratings war, with its football-player type bids for stars and senior management, meant there was a lot of interpenetration. People knew each other – at least the BBC London people and the key men in the five big network commercial companies (the ones who make programmes for national showing: Thames, London Weekend, Granada, Yorkshire and Central. Their Programme Controllers have their own hotline telephone circuit). Once Granada's *World in Action* had *eight* team members who had been at Oxford within the same four years. Lots of these fine youngish folk complained – from time to time – of the political control (call it caution) when a particularly difficult documentary on Northern Ireland, say, was shelved; or when endless manoeuvring wasted or toned down a writer's work.

They complained of a stodgy benevolent monopoly, or of being ruled by the ratings. By and large, however, they did not complain that much. British television was *civilised*. Even when it wasn't, the television families – like civil servants with ministers – brought it into line. The truth is, the television families are a protected species – all that glamour without the vulgarity and the competition. The contractors get a licence – forget printing money, that just follows. And the BBC is official without one having to be like Ministry drudges. The whole thing was blissful compromise. Hot money from double-glazing ads, from entrepreneurs who'd fallen off lorries themselves, buys a Drama Department – or perhaps a Youth Programmes Unit – with vivid, animated girl researchers in pink denim boiler-suits and Kickers. The television families could talk to other television families – the kind grouped round the set knowing there were only four 'real-time' options – programmes on schedules you could read in the *TV* and *Radio Times. Captive audiences.* Video started to spoil it – you didn't know when people watched, or how; and it brought in the Nasties – the blue stuff and the chainsaw killer-driller meat movies. But you could deal with that. What's really frightening is the 'Third Age of TV' notion that all the 'Whither TV?' people are on about. Cable and satellite and outside contractors and all that. What they're saying is, TV is going to be such a big thing that it's going to be no big thing to be in TV. There's not much for the Camelot families in Ted Turner's kind of operation – round the clock news which he sells around like a commodity, in competition with the big national network stations. And as for Ugly George, there's no graduate-training programme there.

That Tuesday night, Kenneth Baker, the Minister for Information Technology, who's not shy of column inches himself, explains the Government's grand intent for a push on cabling this country – thirty stations down the wire by 1986. Two and a half billion sterling on the hardware, great national renewal project, etc, and it's got *her* backing, yes sir. By now the television families are seriously worried, though I hear one senior BBC politician say 'Inside Margaret Thatcher there's Mary Whitehouse, and when she realises it's filth down the line, she'll be edging right back to regulation'. After hours at the festival is fun too – the young independent programme-packagers, hopeful of Channel 4, the last compromise godmother, are harder, smarter, sexier than the protec-

Harold Evans models the Goldcrest Films bowtie look

tors they're hoping to hustle. They're doing the bars like George. In the hotel lounge Ted is talking prices with a British regional contractor: he can do it all so much cheaper. And later in the evening, he is observed showing a young playwright from a feminist group photographs of the Turner spread and the Turner offices – his bears, his bison, his geese, his account executives.

Over in the Scottish Parliament building Granada chairman Sir Denis Forman welcomes one of the first guests to Granada's reception in the Signet Library – Sebastian Graham-Jones, a director, ex-National Theatre, who's working on a new series, so far unnamed, for Granada . . .

'Have you got a title yet?'

'No, but I've got a double-barrelled name.'

Bou-oum.

M·E·N  O·F

# O·U·R   T·I·M·E

March 1982. Perhaps the Princess of Wales is pregnant. On the extended Michael Parkinson show – now broadcast simultaneously in America on the ABC network, Britain (still BBC) and Australia (Kerry Packer's Channel 9), Parkinson has guests from sport, media and fashion. Angela Rippon and Captain Mark Phillips will talk about eventing and their new joint book on it; a short clip from a film on eventing is shown. Barry Mason, the songwriter, describes his new musical *American Heroes* which is to open here shortly. The royal-wedding-dress-makers Liz and David Emanuel have produced a new collection, including a line of baby clothes which has been licensed around the world. Although there is as yet no official word, they are hoping to dress the child because the Princess is a loyal person. They have already said, however, that they will *not talk about that.* There is a short clip of the Emanuels' shows, modelled by some of the star models from the Laraine Ashton agency, including Marie Helvin and Jerry Hall; the hairdressing is by John Frieda, husband of Lulu, an enthusiastic Emanuel customer.

Such a show – it was a fantasy of course – would really have been the Mark McCormack show, an event put together by Mark McCormack, starring McCormack-represented artists and personalities.

Mark Phillips, Angela Rippon, Barry Mason and the Emanuels were all represented by McCormack. Parkinson has been a client of his for ten years. McCormack owns the Laraine Ashton agency and Frieda is another McCormack client, poised for Sassooning outwards into the world. And McCormack of course would have negotiated the deal between the three television companies.

Mark McCormack is usually written up (he has been written up a lot and always has background-briefing press notes to hand in an interview) as an agent, super-agent or, in Yorkshire TV's documentary in 1979, a *Special Agent.* Routinely he is associated with his sports stars – pre-eminently Bjorn Borg – and with huge contracts and deals. More recently he was in the papers, loudly, as organiser of the Pope's visit to England two years ago and, more discreetly, as the new adviser? agent? manager? to the royal dress-making Emanuels. But this conventional perception misses the point of Mark McCormack, a fifty-year-old lawyer (Yale) from Cleveland, Ohio, founder of IMG (International Management Group). McCormack isn't just an agent; he has invented a new kind of American multi-national business – the systematic merchandising of 'personalities' and institutions worldwide.

In a time gone by, American barons owned

# T·H·E   M·A·N   W·H·O

The new capitalism:
Mark McCormack
In Ultra-Planning mode

railroads, coal and steel, but in an age of leisure and celebrity there is room for another kind of capitalism and different commodities. *Agents* find the best buyers, do the best deals for their boys. McCormack isn't as passive as that: he creates the vehicle, the event/race/tournament himself, he turns the stars into a business. If you were a McCormack client property on his 'A' list – the ideal is an *individual* sportsman (not team sports) in a *world* sport (tennis or golf, not baseball or soccer) with long-term earning potential, ideally with no erratic personal or financial affairs – the following things would happen, or have happened. Before being taken on you would, of course, have been assessed for earnings potential and downside risks (moral turpitude, laziness, etc.), and then a notional five-year budget would be calculated. After you joined, your existing contract and obligations – wherever possible – would be renegotiated. *You wouldn't go to the table alone.* The McCormack team would go in there for you; suddenly you would be a corporation. They would establish that you had profit potential, but other options and suitors too – yesterday Mark was talking to X in Italy, tomorrow to Y in Japan.

The IMG would act to put on a world stage, out of the parochialism of the little UK and would sell you worldwide, license your image here for sportswear, there for ghosting books, somewhere else for a retail shop-within-a-shop. And you will go into *media*. This doesn't mean publicity – it means probably that you will go into a film or video organised by McCormack's films division, you will make a series of them, in Australia or Timbuktu. If you are hot enough, interviews with you will be treated as *performance* – the media will buy you. Certainly rights to photographs of you will be restricted and *sold*. If the McCormack assessment is right, this process will at least treble or quadruple your income once it is in gear. IMG will deal with tax. It lays stress on tax-planning, planning from the word go, since it sets up the deals and collects the money. This means changing one's way of life. A major 'A' list person will probably have to change 'domicile' and go into tax exile. Tax planning is just part of the financial package, however; you will be invested for. And round the clock, if you're a real 'A', they will find people to do things for you: houses will be cleaned, travel arranged, flowers sent to wives – a plethora of Universal Aunts services.

The cost of these services will not be standard. Certainly it is more than ten per cent of what they earn for you, one hears twenty per cent, one hears thirty-five. A deal has to be struck or an 'association' formed between you and IMG. How you

# S·E·L·L·S   T·H·E   W·O·R·L·D

The Pope limbering up to open another Olympic merchandising campaign for Mark McCormack

joined them depends too. If you're an A-potential talent in an activity that really matters to IMG, you will have been monitored and approached by McCormack, who will have kept files on you since for ever. At the margins, you will have approached him, gone cap in hand saying 'Make me rich'. The total of clients is impressive, however.

In the *old* system of celebrity – still working in many old personality industries where McCormack's flow production has not been introduced – a famous person could have as many as seven people working for him. He could have, typically, a manager, an agent, a lawyer, a PR man, a licensing agent, an investment counsellor and a tax lawyer, all working for different firms – all potential sources of conflict and inefficiency. When McCormack goes in he may just agree to retain, as he says, 'someone's uncle who has been acting as accountant for fifteen years', but you can see he doesn't like it. IMG really means Integrated Management. 'Sports-leisure', as they call it in the business magazines, is now producing stars as big as the movies do – bigger perhaps, more modern, more *merchandisable*. Under McCormack's management Arnold Palmer (his first client) and Borg have certainly become safe millionaires. Many other clients are alleged millionaires or on their way. The McCormack publicity provides a flow of six-figure deals, seven-figure deals. *This man, so the story goes, can make you rich.*

It has certainly made McCormack rich, but more than that, it has built a real business; 400 people in real offices around the world (the quoted turnover – $50 million – seems to understate its size). It began less glamorously, in the very early sixties, with golf and Arnold Palmer. McCormack used his legal training to help Palmer, his friend and partner in a number of ventures, make money out of the rights to himself. There was Arnold Palmer everything – even an Arnold Palmer hotel. McCormack learnt along the way that those business-school slogans about the coming 'leisure age' meant ... *sports merchandising*. He was in at the beginning and spotted when sport switched from team and fantasy sports (baseball, boxing) to sport as therapy for all (golf, tennis). It was a new field,

so 'total management' was the obvious approach.

By 1965 he had Jack Nicklaus and Gary Player too, and the act was rolling. And McCormack understood business, just like the corporate lawyer he would otherwise have become. *McCormack understood corporate USA*. It was run by people like himself – big blond Ivy League, good old boys trained in law and business, but not *too* North-eastern or flashy (the slightly dour greyness of industrial Cleveland, Ohio, was a background

Love doubles: Mr and Mrs John Lloyd, Bjorn Borg and Mariana Simionescu

Craggy jazz-loving Yorkshire ex-sports writer and Australian TV chat show host Michael Parkinson, a McCormack artiste

plus-point for him). He didn't have the craft ethic, or the narrow view of old Hollywood or Broadway agents. Mainstream multi-national corporate USA and its huge promotional budgets were his obvious targets.

So McCormack got the corporate USA and later the corporate world to sponsor every last inch of his boys. Over the last twenty years sponsorship itself, like advertising before, has been a huge growth area. Business puts money into sport, the

Ian Wooldridge, *Daily Mail* sports columnist, another McCormack artiste

arts, etc, to redeem itself ('social hygiene' it's called in the trade); to create a new kind of advertising or get round the restrictions on the old kind (cigarettes, liquor); or simply to reward its top management with the ultimate perk ... access to celebrity. The board likes to meet the Big Boys.

McCormack was in there at the beginning of the sponsorship boom too. So one corporation would be making his celebrities' widgets (golf clubs, etc.) under licence, while another used his boys in their commercials, and another put their name on the tennis court tournament or slapped it across a car bonnet. McCormack's growth years were the multi-national media years too: satellite television, international co-productions. Sponsored television films and video became international commodities, sports coverage went up, *international brands* could be truly international with simultaneous transmission. Be on the right hoarding when the cameras swung and you'd get into hundreds of millions of homes worldwide.

*Rights*, control of rights, subsidiary rights, licensing rights, sponsorships, exclusivities: McCormack's business was built on balancing exposure against control. IMG's stars are never exploited by paparazzi or intrusive TV cameras, their images will not adorn unlicensed ash trays in Mexico or kiddies' tennis-rackets in Nigeria: the rights have been assigned.

McCormack's collection of interests and companies have made this approach easier. He does not represent just talents – 'artistes' – but often the events that show-case them. Thus he negotiates the rights to Wimbledon's television exposure with the BBC. He doesn't just put people into film, he runs what he claims is the world's largest independent sports-film company, Trans World International, which produces the *Superstars* series on BBC1, which naturally enough includes McCormack's own greats (Bjorn Borg, Jackie Stewart).

He doesn't just have talents, but 'communicators' like Rippon and Parkinson and, by all accounts, wants more of them. Interlinked activities can amortise the talents still further. This is what, in the corporate language, is called *vertical integration*, and the rubbing together of two legally related sticks is called 'synergy'. Thus such genius strokes of McCormack's as the Mark Phillips/Angela Rippon book on three-day eventing. He is royal, she can write, both are McCormack clients.

Now McCormack is moving out of sports – cautiously, never sacrificing his base – but looking to build up fashion, media, entertainment. 'Not pop stars,' he tells me, 'they can be erratic, they have very complicated affairs ... but if *Paul McCartney* were to come to me ...' His eyes light up.

Fashion is more logical than it seems if you have lots of clothing contacts already (sportswear). Why not a designer under licence as well? And communications is, well, logical. Mark is a communicator himself – he commentates ably, on events like the Open golf championship in July. These businesses have a common *modus operandi*. But not politics. Shutters down when I asked him about politics. He doesn't see politics as an area of development. Despite his caution, the new developments have raised flak – the first real flak he has had in a while (the professionalisation-of-sport debate is over now). The coverage of McCormack's assignment to handle merchandising for the papal visit was predictable and, all considered, mild, directed as much at the Church as anything else. The general feel was: here's a pretty brassy gang. His signing-up of the Emanuels produced a different delayed reaction. Word *flew* round the fashion press that McCormack was charging for an interview with the Emanuels. Then *Private Eye* had a story saying the *International Herald Tribune's grande dame*, Hebe Dorsay, had been asked £2,500 for an interview. This was culture shock. The couture, particularly royal couture, didn't behave like that. The Princess, so the story ran, had said to a friend she hoped the dress wouldn't say 'Wimbledon' across the back. Gossip coverage of the Emanuels turned sour – 'grasping frock-makers' was the usual term.

McCormack's personal style is not half so brassy as it is projected. He looks what he is, a corporation lawyer animated by a stroke of nutty genius and a twitch. He dresses reasonably, save for a suggestion of double-knit in the trousers (one has

seen pictures of lurid golf outfits). He looks like a handsomer Jimmy Carter: the same colouring, faded blond. Regaining health and control after a serious illness eight years ago seems an obsession for him: he has many of those *control* fetishes of American corporation men – jogging, monitoring his time-use – but to an extreme. He double-tracks, i.e. he will be holding a perfectly good interview conversation with you, and monitoring his secretary's telephone call in the hallway, and planning the day ahead. He doesn't talk disc-jockey booster talk – his speech is careful, yet impatient, logical and legal (words like 'monies' and 'defray' crop up constantly). Perfectly civilised. He is not a man troubled by doubt, either. His imperatives seem conventional ones: extend, diversify, amortise. The imagination comes out in the events – the 'love doubles' which netted tennis (ex-) couples like the Lloyds an alleged $80,000 for an exhibition match.

What you think of McCormack depends on your reactions to American mainstream business. McCormack's critics see his business as monopolistic, making sport unfree; they see the synergy between McCormack activities and talents as sinister. At another level, the fashion business experiences culture shock, and his relationships with royalty and God seem an odd conjunction. They would rather not know about the financing of the mystic. People with a trade ethic are worried by IMG, because it appears to be a business machine with no respect for boundaries. Journal-

Mr and Mrs David Emanuel wait to join the team

ists on the 'quality' papers tend not to like the McCormack concept – it is often described as a 'ruthless' operation, though little chapter and verse have been produced. McCormack, indeed IMG generally, appears unworried. What the *Eye* reveals, they tell you cheerfully, incredulous at the criticism, is just business. So what if the *Daily Mail's* Sports Feature Editor, Ian Wooldridge, presenter of Yorkshire TV's mythically styled 1979 documentary on *McCormack Special Agent*, is now a McCormack client and has married McCormack's London PA, Sarah.

So what if McCormack is commentating on his own players at times. And communicators like Nigel Dempster (see 'The one that got away', below) are just merchandisable talent like any other. As for 'ruthless', he may be rough and tough on the juniors, but his top men and his PAs tend to stay on and internalise his style. He is said to be loyal to friends. IMG attributes criticism to jealousy or inefficiency. McCormack sees his effects in cautious terms: 'What we have generally done has been pretty successful and pretty good quality.' And The Boys get to spend a lot of time in Monte Carlo.

## The one that got away

In Wedding Year Nigel Dempster appeared on Thames TV's *Afternoon Plus* show with McCormack's new signings, the Emanuels. 'I got £60 for being a hundred times more amusing and intelligent than the Emanuels, whose one contribution was to say that Diana Spencer would not wear jeans for the wedding. The Emanuels got £4,000.' (McCormack had negotiated for a joint showing on the American NBC network.) McCormack had actually wanted Dempster as a client. 'John Webber told me in February, "Mark wants to expand his interests in your world".' An offer followed with a contract suggestion. Dempster, however, could not see the advantage in it. 'All they would have been doing is taking money for no benefit. I'd have had to work like a dog to pay their percentage – I can't endorse things ... everyone knows you've gone then.'

Angela Rippon joins the McCormack chorus line

# F·I·L·M  G·I·R·L

Who is she, this quietly charismatic woman from humble provincial origins who has risen to a position of unparalleled influence on today's young people, with her clarion calls for a return to traditional – or, as she would describe it, classical – values? Julie Burchill's sympathies are a challenge to the liberal sloppiness of the late sixties and early seventies.

Julie Burchill believes in the family, in Britain and her people, and in the Commonwealth. She is intensely patriotic, after her fashion, and was deeply affected by the Falklands. She is concerned to restore Law and Order, in particular capital punishment. She admires Ian Paisley and counts among her heroes such people as the late Arthur Harris (Bomber Command) and the late Lord Mountbatten. Her beliefs are based on intense feeling for history and geography. She loves animals. Conversely she opposes the pet causes of the 'rebel'-loving Left establishment – the excessive concern with the 'civil rights' of such people as muggers and other criminals, homosexuals and the IRA (all the groups of causes she identifies with the singularly misled Ken Livingstone). She is, in short, a conservative authoritarian who sees much of the rebel culture of the post-war years, and the liberal arts ghetto that has fostered it, as a juvenile aberration that has put the immutable moral laws in jeopardy. She is untroubled by doubt. She has, after all, been considering those questions since she was 11. She would say, rather like that port advertisement, that *one instinctively knows when something is right.* This soft-spoken young housewife and mother not surprisingly puts some observers in mind of the most popular and most published aspects of the Prime Minister's world-view.

There are, however, certain subtle differences of outlook, perhaps reflecting differences of generation and circumstances (Julie Burchill – in private life Mrs Anthony Parsons – is 25, the PM 58). Julie is anti-nuclear, pro-Soviet, and anti-American.

Her affection for animals means Animal Liberation. Her form of patriotism meant turning out against the National Front in the great Lewisham scuffle. Before Julie was 17, so she says, she had never met a non-working-class person apart from *teachers.* After that, however, they were all over her. Hardly a day passes now without some sweet young bourgeois liberal wishing to recruit her and her novelist husband Tony to some Left-spectrum political party or pressure group, wishing to interview her or somehow wishing to add some aspect of her most attractive personality and appearance to their lives. Demanding and contradictory though her views may be, they know that she is the most singular, vigorous and influential young writer in this country and it would be useful to have her endorse their cause. Thus Paul Foot (SWP), Tom Robinson (Gay Lib) and Ray Gosling (over-forties rebel party).

Since she left a Bristol technical college at 17 to come to London and write essays for the *New Musical Express* (weekly worldwide circulation about 130,000) it has been quite obvious that there is no one like her. The rock press has by definition little room for history, for the mainstream of English culture, for the things that move the public heartbeat or for what is *genuinely* popular (for the rock press view of the working class is usually somewhat confused). Or for women; for the rock press serves the interests and sensibility of boys. In this context Julie Burchill, a girl, genuinely working-class (rather than highly educated sunken middle-class seeking roots) and with an enormous and surprising range of cultural references from Stalin to Stella Gibbons's Seth Starkadder, stood out from day one.

You had to re-read her pieces to be absolutely sure that she'd actually *said* it. There she was making judgements *from a moral standpoint* ('a worthless person', 'a degraded man', and so on) and showing an extraordinary conjunction of real understanding of the modern popular culture (committed Leftists usually get these things wrong) with a thoroughly perverse sense of humour; usually that of a woman laughing at little boys being Big Babies; she was *the* writer.

Her first book, *The Boy Looked at Johnny*, written with Tony Parsons, was a diatribe against the rock/rebel culture. I don't think it represents her style adequately but it has, ironically enough, affected the thinking of young bourgeois, etc, thinkers in many Western countries where it is . . . a cult book. Her second, *Girls on Film*, was a mature, attractive work covering the recurrent themes of her writing: *beauty* – to her a form of nostalgia – Communism, and history, all in a way that merited the attention of more than just the Large Format Paperback type of person.

It took nearly seven years for mainstream Fleet Street to discover her. For the quality press, the rock press world wasn't quite *real*. They only recruited her – to the *Sunday Times* as an occasional columnist on the Look pages – when they'd read about her in their own Court Circulars, magazines that Sunday paper women's editors read. She started wonderfully, with the best calculated insult around to all the professional women journalists – what she called, Career Cows or Female Impersonators – an attack on female friendship. It was heaven, meaning Fleet Street could see a truly modern Jean Rook in the making, with credibility too. They called her the *punk* columnist, of course, as if it meant something to them. Unsurprisingly enough, some Fleet Street old lags like Suzanne Lowry saw her as unpleasantly *reactionary*. Underground, overground, she hadn't lost the talent to annoy. She understood, instinctively, the mind-set of the Islington Oxbridge educated career wife as well as the 1977 Rock Cretin. Next time she went on to explain that drug dealers were fine, it was the ghastly pushy addicts who should be put down. She was interviewed in *Time Out* and confessed she might be losing her faith in the working classes since they were so apathetic. What if the ghastly Paul Johnson was right? What if Auberon Waugh had a point? She came right out and said that too. Will she be received into the New Right Alternative Comedy-Brotherhood, take Instruction at Farm Street, perhaps winter with Harold Acton, or visit America as a Guggenheim Fellow? An international audience of pen-pals awaits.

Julie Birchill in the classic 1978 Pennie Smith photograph, now her logo

Bryan on a nice repro
Chippendale chair in a nice
jacket of West End cut with cuff
detail and a proper bowtie

# B·R·Y·A·N'S
# I·N·T·E·R·I·O·R

### Mr B. Ferry and Miss L. Helmore

The marriage took place quietly on 26 June 1982 at
the Church of St Anthony and St George, Duncton,
Sussex, between Mr Bryan Ferry and
Miss Lucy Helmore.

A lot of people were worried about Bryan's interior. Worried and puzzled. A lot had bought the first edition of *Interiors* just for Bryan, of course (clever old Min Hogg to get him to do it, clever PR to tell the world). More people than one realised had the Life of Bryan preying on their minds. It would start – a complete *non sequitur* – from ad men in their thirties; brilliant beautiful teenage girls . . . stylists of all kinds came out with it.

They felt Bryan had let them down. They had no idea exactly what they'd been expecting, but certainly not this. They didn't understand the chintz, the Turkey carpet, the grey taffeta and the Aubusson. It left them inexplicably depressed. They thought it was . . . dull. And they thought he'd left them for somewhere else, finally broken with downtown. I can't tell you. I must have had this conversation maybe eight times over. This was about the same time that the gossip columns were

generally starting to cover the Lucy Helmore side of the Life of Bryan and Lucy, by contrast with the spectaculars he'd had before – Jerry Hall, Marilyn Cole, Amanda Lear, whom most stories didn't dwell on, and Kari-Ann Moller (now Mrs Chris Jagger) who'd said in the *Sunday Mirror* that he put her on a pedestal and made her the inspiration of his songs – Lucy was determinably, from her photographs, a Sloane Ranger, albeit good-looking.

And Bryan's previous places, well, the Notting Hill Gate house, even the Earl's Court flat, had all had something a bit spectacular about them, a bit of a twist, a touch of the *avant-gardes*, something kitschy, ironic, something to set you wondering, a surprise.

So they'd been expecting, hoping against hope, that Bryan would give them a lead, a glimmer for the eighties. And here instead, so they said, was this stiff, correct flat, with its carefully chosen things, apparently designed for an inhibited elderly upper-middle-class aesthete. You couldn't see them doing it on that floor. Backwards into the future, forwards into the past, and perhaps a little step to the right. Bryan, they suddenly suspected, was serious about this stuff.

Of course Bryan had always had a particular following – though it had become a bit diluted over the years. Anyone who'd had a severe disturbance of the eye had seen Bryan as the Second Coming in 1972. There are perfectly sane men and women who will tell you that those first Rainbow Roxy Music concerts changed their lives; the presentation, the cleverness, the stylisation, the audience (Roxy Music invented the audience-as-star-stylist syndrome). It was as if Post-Modern Art School style had burst its banks, taken over the world. They looked marvellous then: futurist revivalist. The words were unbelievably clever, Bryan obviously understood the RCA, St Martin's, Brighton, Hockney, Notting Hill, Andy and everything that mattered, the whole Modern World. (Of course, as we all know now, BA Fine Arts Newcastle, studied under Richard Hamilton.) It was merely a bonus for this crowd that the music was equally brilliant, innovative. The first two Roxy albums are still a revelation.

The real thing was the identification which a lot of troubled boys took a long way in 1973 to 1975, wearing complete Bryan kits to early concerts – hair flopping over one eye and tuxedo, GI kit or whatever. A lot was emotionally invested in Bryan – men, it can be done – more than many ostensibly bigger stars. It was a great burden, analogous to, but subtly different in practice from, that carried by his contemporary, David Bowie. Between them they did the groundwork for the eighties. They both seemed to endorse their fans, brave nervous kids who thought they'd found someone for them after the hideous desert of the late sixties (the terrible wallies – the Joe Cockers and Yeses and Frees – the rock world was unbelievably naff). These dreamers of the Golden Dream.

They'd stuck with him as he started to make real money, moved out of Earl's Court because, in the

Bryan in check shirt counterpoints a new mood in interior decoration. Dentil cornice marks the Post-Modern divide from the studio

*Right* Bryan recaptures his mid-seventies *tuxedo* mode for French photographers in 1982

*Below* Among the creatures of the night in Anthony Price's crucial GI look in 1975 (still widely imitated)

classic ghetto way, he was doing it for them. Those spectacular girls; that stylisation; those magazine spreads with Ferry – that was what you did with hot new money. You patronised the new, the glamorous. The people never resent serious glamour – good luck to him, they say. And whatever he did, it was just a look. The taste thing wasn't a problem yet. And the Chelsea social side of things, that was surely a kind of send-up. It seemed conventional but then again, maybe not. It seemed like a very clever uptown/downtown dialogue.

The press was fairly late on to the central theme in the Life of Bryan, the obsessive fastidiousness which, not surprisingly, meant he loathed the mainstream music business and its appalling

A severe
neo-classical
corner of
the studio

clothes and manners and, equally, was drawn to the tone-on-tone subtleties of traditional rich aesthetes. Ferry is the only popular music star to have mastered the visual grammar of Jermyn Street, the only one ever to have worn a real tweed jacket.

So after he'd done Café Society (from 1974 to 1977) he started on the real thing; rather in the

manner of, say, Noel Coward or Fred Astaire. In an earlier age people would merely have said that he had found his own level. He was rich, handsome, well-educated and well-mannered, why should he not knock around on the country-house circuit if he wished? (In the late seventies, one would meet totally crusty people who said they'd just met a delightful pop star in the country, not what they'd expected at all, so quiet and well-mannered. It was always Bryan.) He had defended it intelligently and quietly when challenged, saying that he believed in 'social exploration' and that he was not, after all, public property except on stage – why should he be bound by the inverted snobbery of the plain and unadventurous? If Jermyn Street was good, why not have it? But it was against the temper of the times, against the clichés of the music business.

And the exploration seemed very much one-way. Difficult to swallow, difficult to follow, for the stylists could barely imagine Country House, let alone aspire to it. Trousers and attitude, Bryan, that's what counts on the club floor.

The late seventies were hard for Bryan. Punk made him look – temporarily – back-dated. Jerry Hall leaving made him look a loser. He really suffered and, because he is tough and disciplined, he plotted. He was at No. 1 for the first time in 1981 and Roxy Music have made more money in the last few years than in all the *succès d'estime* period. Bryan has become mainstream, acceptable in the adult-oriented catologue beside Diana Ross and Manhattan Transfer.

He is married, settled, even has a son, put down for Eton. Lives have cycles and Bryan is now grown-up. And the art school kids, the misfits from the outer suburbs, today's dreamers of the Golden Dream, now have a new generation of enthusiasms, all of whom, fifteen years younger, have absorbed Bryan's perspective, singing intonations and musical tricks in their cradles – but they jump about more. Meanwhile, the Father of the Post-Modern remains in Chelsea with the portrait of Ottoline Morrell and the Edwardian girl in the manner of Sargent, as if the tacky seventies – never mind the sixties – had never been.

S·M·A·L·L

O·F

A·N·D

MATTERS

GROOMING

DEPORTMENT

# T·H·E
# V·O·I·C·E

If lizards could talk they'd have the Voice. Staring back at you from a minimal rock in their lizard skins with their lizard eyes, psyching you out, being unimpressed:

'Do we ha-ave to?' It'll come right back at you, talking from a whole long way away, 'D'you mind terr-ibly if I don't come?' The Voice will rain on anyone's parade.

'Oh re-ally,' the Voice says quite a lot, and you know where it got *that*. Indeed it's the most familiar thing about the Voice, this New York Minimal Voice – if you're English that is. The English – meaning English upper-middle – say 'oh rairly' – and depending on *how*, it can mean absolutely anything in the world. True Preps sound to me as if they're saying something like 'oh rilly' and the Voice, coming out of the lizard as old as time itself says 'oh rear-lly'. Which means just one thing (for-get it, it's *finished*).

The Voice was practically the first thing I met in America when I came to do New York in the early seventies with some artsy fashiony media introductions. You'd call the people on your little list and – every time a blood orange as we say – you'd get the Voice asking you to call back later, saying it was *wonder-ful* that I'd arrived but it was going to the Hamptons that very day.

I was spellbound; could a whole alternative nation of people speak just so *flat* – it was so very different from the Americans I saw on morning TV who *screamed* – literally went ape – when they won on game shows networked from the West Coast. Like most little English people I had seen some Andy films, knew about superstars and the aesthetic of boredom. But I'd never *met* any Voice-carrying members.

I used to get confused between my Voices on the telephone – and sometimes embarrassingly, about the sex of them. The Voice does not discriminate. It wasn't just gays; women and straights have the Voice. Anyone who's been through the process has the Voice. The Voice has been bleached by experience so the men have this amazing neuter flatness, and the women too. Sometimes the women sounded a bit more *gravelly*: the Voice has left gender behind; hence the mistakes.

The Voice was hard going; I'd be explaining some little British enthusiasm and it'd tell me how X's current performances were just a *joke*; how Y had never made it in New York, and how Z never would. The Voice always knew; it had friends in the business, it knew all *those* people. The Voice sometimes called one Peder-darling which meant *I can barely remember your name.*

I couldn't cope with the Voice – there was absolutely nothing to lock on to – except the put-downs. The absolute flatness, the *affectlessness* meant you couldn't see behind it at all – what did these people want? How had they got that way? Back in London I would imitate the Voice – though you couldn't keep the flatness going for long – to see who friends thought it was. Junkies or Seventh Avenue people they seemed to think – Seventh Avenue junkies.

The origins of the Voice – ironically because today the Voice couldn't love the status quo more – seem to be in some highly un-American activities; the drug voice meant 'I'm so far away you can't touch me'; the ethnic tough bitch wise-cracking voice said no quarter given and none taken; the New York fag voice said 'oh c'mon'. Irony and distance and we-can-take-it toughness was New York. Of course, I didn't know New York itself was an un-American activity then.

The Voice drew on druggie and toughie and gay styles to forge an adoptive Manhattan occupational tone for the sixties, That was when New York first started to develop a really profitable Uptown/Downtown social dialogue. And the genius behind the voice, of course, was Andy. Warhol created a whole set of ideas that came out in the Voice; the irony, the disingenuousness, the fake enthusiasms (the Voice only enthuses when you're meant to know it doesn't mean it). The Voice was the perfect weapon to psyche out just about anyone – but particularly middle-brow media types.

 Psyching out was what the Voice was all about. The Voice withheld just about everything, approval, interest, clues. The Voice was defensive too, a great vocal transit camp for voices that rilled or gushed or had some kind of bridge and tunnel or Hicktown overtones. The Voice washed all that away, bleached and pumiced it down to minimal. What these people were doing was rejecting the sheer embarrassing *effusiveness* of first-generation American prosperity for the New York style statement of the sixties and early seventies. 'Less is more.' This solved a lot of social mobility problems, since the real traditional East Coast upper-class voice is just about the most inaccessible sound on earth. The minimal Voice was a more modern alternative. But the Voice still included elements of what it saw as grand – the hauteur, the world-weariness and the put-downs all came from an idea of how the world's aristos carried on. There might have been a certain confusion between Brooke Astor and Mary Astor but the aristocratic principle was in there somewhere. For Ease substitute the Freeze. The middlebrow art-critical types got reams of copy out of Andy Style but what a raft of less fanciful types got was the Attitude, the turns of Phrase, and the Voice. The Voice took off like crazy in the commercial arts – retailing and fashion and design and magazine-land among people who'd never done more than a little grass, would never know an art theory if it hit them in the face – who, in short, wouldn't have begun to understand half of the Factory ramifications. But the sound and the tricks solved a lot of problems. The Voice implied that its owner had done it – from Diana Vreeland to the Mineshaft to Milan – just like that. Probably on the same day. The Voice said it wasn't from New Jersey or Somewhereville Texas but from that special self-invented New York Social World.

In time the Voice devolved upon the rest of America and one would meet media girls and designer men in other very different cities who spoke just so. Today the Voice is, well, really rather establishment – certainly, but certainly, not radical – and just a little bit period.

This is ironic because the Voice believes above all in the transforming power of fashion and novelty. The Voice's younger brother and sister aren't quite so inhibited – or so defensive. They don't mind a bit of enthusiasm – it's actually rather fashionable, they don't need all that cool to be distant, because American life has cooled down a whole lot anyway. They don't need to act blank – about all that inherited moral baggage, all that naïve prosperity – if their parents had done acid and read *Rolling Stone* now, they *are* blank. Light and shade, *Maximal*, Sunbelt Style, everything piled in high relief on the plate, as messy and expressionist as you like, that's what they want.

# T·H·E  G·L·I·N·T

*Staying Alive* was *the* Glint movie. It had Glinting Stallone, Tribune of the People, directing; Glinting Travolta, with the Born-Again brain and body rediscovering his past (ie the movie that made him) and *the* theme, the eternal Fame/Glint theme – one's incredible always-been-there talent recognised on the night through the Artistic Medium of the Dance; it was perfect. Actually it was a ghastly humourless thing, after the wonderful *Saturday Night Fever*, but it gave us a laugh, because of all the high-wattage Glints everyone was putting out. The Glint shines out in performance; in interviews and on chat shows when some essential part of the personality is replaced by one of those new *self-actualising* micro-chips.

In science-fiction movies of the late fifties/early sixties this was always happening – the hero would be talking to his old friend, regular Bob/Dick and notice ... an *inappropriate response* – you know, something like an inability to get a downhome joke, or notice when a cigarette was burning his hand. Looking at Bob's eyes gleaming over his shoulder into Up There, he'd realise that Bob had *gone* ... had been taken over.

The Glint can start just about anywhere ... It's modern life. If you watch a lot of TV you can spend many happy hours as a Glint monitor, waiting for the moment when, say, an actress describes how *personal growth* has enabled her to tackle a more serious part or a sportsman says he doesn't want to be pretentious, but the sport is an Art Form (or he's done it through Pyramid Power). Righteous Glinting comes through if you write a fitness handbook (the British press had a wonderful time with Victoria Principal, as she Glinted her way through chat shows and press conferences spreading the grooming vocation. The fitness people have after all cleared out the temple of the soul).

The Glinters also have a *Psychic Wing*; when you hear a country and western singer explain her belief in reincarnation – *in another life Johnny I was an Egyptian Princess* – then you know some serious Glinting's going on. Mr Murjani of Gloria Vanderbilt seemed to sparkle a bit to me, when he described how he'd let God in to oversee the Empire of the Swan. One felt he was into destiny.

Fertility arouses massive Glinting in women who think they're too good for it. Self-discovery through motherhood, as described on TV by a novelist become Corn Goddess, through the

Dolly Parton with the blessed Arnold:
perhaps a trifle too existentialist now?

sacrifice of themselves and a famous figure for nine months to produce ... an extrusion ... is a Glint classic. This particular drama of motherhood Glints its way to the bank on Johnny Carson and in *People* every month.

Sudden Social Success has much the same effect; when Steve Rubell was a Roman Emperor at Studio 54, orbiting the entrée, his interviews revealed him as positively incandescent. Promoted gossip columnists move from the merely star-struck careerist to a sense of Mission astonishingly quickly – they see themselves as serious dispensers of a kind of social justice ('I wasn't going to let "X" get away with what she said to "W",' they would say, lasers raking the Côte Basque over your shoulder). It becomes *freedom of the press* that the readers should know who had a quickie divorce in Mexico or a nip and tuck in Brazil.

The Glint is all about Self. When self-assertion becomes manifest, destiny and media and mobility shepherd it toward the light – the arc light of the Big Interview when just being yourself becomes something astonishingly spiritual. The Glint strikes when you believe what you've read about yourself, particularly those seminal articles that discover something a bit *deep, contradictory, ironic, symbolic of a major social trend, or an important group of people* in you. Something that says you're *more* than a hoofer, a crooner, a runner, or a haberdasher. The Glint hits when you get Media Biofeedback, when you incorporate this aspect of yourself as an 'interesting person' in your next interview. I was very worried when the otherwise wonderful Dolly Parton started peddling that line about how it cost a fortune to look so trashy, as if her poor white background was some kind of existentialist marketing ploy. She'd been reading her coverage in the uptown press.

The Glint, one has to say, is particularly American. The peasant evangelical tradition and the modern me-ism has combined to produce born-again-ness, a word only available on import in Britain. And American media, *at every level* (just check out the literary monthlies) thrusts forward to evoke the perfect artefact of personality,

*Above* John Travolta perceives his manifest destiny in 'Staying Alive': the eyes have it

*Opposite* Sylvester Stallone, Tribune of the People, among them

the Hyper-Glint. There's no inhibiting layer of irony or reticence.

The people of Britain are often puzzled when occasionally they read about a Mrs Vreeland, who appears to be an elderly lady of Red Indian origins. Are the references to her wonderfulness — taste, discrimination, Zeitgeisting, etc. — part of some high-society integration scheme? Was she perhaps on the musical stage — there is no record of her appearance in *Cabin in the Sky*, *Showboat* or *Soldier Blue*? We haven't seen her duet with Andy Williams. Who exactly is she? Whoever she is, it would be remarkable if she hadn't developed one of the greatest Glints of all time after what's been

written about her (association with any *art* institution, incidentally, provokes more Glint than anything on earth, namely the realisation that anything one does can be *looked at another way, as art*).

The reality of Glint is this: in *Being There* the Peter Sellers character is a simple soul — people just read things into him — and he stays that way. In the real world he'd be catching Merv Griffith's TV eye with his Glint, explaining how he'd always been a simple person; how he knew folks knew they could trust him because he was a simple person and that simple didn't mean dumb because, after all Merv ... less *means more*.

*Below left* That Fairisle feeling: Hovis advertising conceived by deep Fairisle fanciers Geoff Seymour and Frank Lowe in Howland Street, W1, set in the West Country, representing Edwardian Lancashire   *Below right* Hamlet cigars: the 1920s Fairisle-vet look sicklied o'er with the pale cast of studio wardrobe: ensemble includes Norfolk jacket in brownish herringbone with interesting raised seam detail and designer-look bowtie   *Right* All the lonely Fairisles, where do they all come from? Poignant Paul in pained pose   *Far right* Fairisle, plus-fours, Argyll socks and correspondent shoes in Ken Russell's 'Fairisle Friend': Russell started the Fairisle Film School in the mid-sixties

# T·H·E  F·A·I·R·I·S·L·E  Y·E·A·R·S

*The Jewel in the Crown* wasn't a Fairisle film, I couldn't see a Fairisle anywhere. You could say *too warm* but I don't think that'd have held them back if they'd really wanted one in – Barbie could've hauled one out of her trunk as a relic of one of her little charges or Hari Kumar could've been seen wearing one in a Chillingborough flashback. It must mean something. Fairisle films started, well probably at the back end of the sixties and even before, with Ken Russell, but the high-point of the genre was *Cabaret*, which put the Fairisle slipover on a world stage. That must have been about the same time Edina and Lena started selling the real old ones in the Antiquarius market in the King's Road – 1971-ish. After that the Fairisle Brotherhood affected almost everything – not just Fairisle films but Fairisle TV and Fairisle commercials. We used to do a Fairisle count; the first to do a five-bar-gate – five separate Fairisles in a week – got a silly prize.

Fairisle starred in an impressive list of feature films like *Chariots of Fairisle*, major TV series like *Fairisle Vet* and award-winning commercials like the Hovis spectacular 'Fairisle memories'. (Did you know that Fairisle Films' chairman, David Puttnam, is never seen in public without his lucky Fairisle slipover – *never*.)

The Fairisle view of art history is somewhere between D.H. Lawrence and L.S. Lowry, the North that never was – like Paul McCartney in a grandad collarless shirt with a Fairisle. That's Hovis Fairisle. But there's the Bertie Wooster School of Fairisle too. The kind you see in one of these Agatha Christie adaptations starring Penelope Keith (the designers get it muddled with Argyll which was very *Prince of Wales*). In the early seventies art

students used to wear thirties Isherwood traveller kit, baggy tweed trousers, Fairisle and a bow-tie.

There's no telling the number of *periods* Fairisle can usefully cover; in the new Provincial Teenage Embarrassment films, all set in the fifties and sixties – the kind where lovers of 19 don't know how to kiss – the hero always has a home-knitted Fairisle. Fairisle is the *Ploughman's Lunch* of sweaters, all ages of innocence at one go.

Fairisle has everything really, it's folk, it's fairly ethnic – like our very own Red Indian knitters – it's period; its provincial or posh (*you* lived in Fairisle and little kilts as a girl in Wiltshire, didn't you, Caroline . . . ). A Fairisle can add such a lift to a young GLC planner's Man at C & A suit; it shows several kinds of sympathy all at the same time; warmth without weight.

The Fairisle, in short is a barometer of the sensi-tive younger middle-aged mind in this country. In strong Fairisle periods there is a flourishing of British creativity – meaning finance is available for period films with heavy wardrobe interest – and in weak ones tower blocks fall down and Mrs Thatcher has trouble with her legs. That is why we cannot afford to let market forces rule and allow Korean imitations to compete in world markets.

The recent Arts Council redeployment – other-wise so sensible – failed to take the obvious course that would be followed by any other NATO country – namely to slap a preservation order on the Fairisles – wherever they might be – give the knitters proper grants, as primitive artists, set up minimum standards, and commission a Fairisle tapestry of British post-war triumphs to hang in little Stephen Bayley's attractive white-tiled Museum of Design in the V & A.

## THE FAIRISLE YEARS

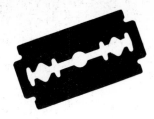

# N·O·T  S·H·A·V·I·N·G

I blame Jack Nicolson for the Not Shaving. He was the first person I can remember in *Major* magazine profile colour spreads, shot by *Major* photographers in sessions taking days and many thousands of dollars fixed up by PR people, earning not less than $75,000 pa to be ... Not Shaved. But he wasn't the only one, there's a whole raft of *serious* middle-aged movie actors who made it in the late sixties/early seventies and go around being Not Shaved in their posed confrontations with the press. I mean the Hoffman, Pacino, De Niro type of actor. The type of person who might be described as, say, surprisingly intelligent and thoughtful, or articulate or something like that – i.e. anything but a dumb blonde. Not Shaving seemed to be a way of saying they had authenticity, accessibility, vulnerability etc. and didn't care too much about appearances.

The idea, I imagine, was that you'd be able to identify with them better if you were a bit short of hot water and Gillette Foamy yourself. Oh, sweet Marie Antionette fantasies when you're getting $1,000,000 a picture. They didn't Not Shave for their first mid-sixties auditions when they lived in shared cold-water walk-up apartments way downtown. It's now they've got five-bathroom homes they don't shave.

Superstar Not Shaving is a miracle of logistics; it's *always* at two days, never the dirty smear of one day after, or the impending straggle of four, but always at a particular length ... an aesthetic convention. How is this arranged – is it specially trimmed – hair by hair – by Chinese girls who make house calls in LA? Do people like this live two days on, two off? It's a mystery.

Behind the Not Shaving was a whole set of new leisure-class display conventions for the seventies represented by these wholefood actors, owing a bit

Dustin Hoffman takes it to a length auditioning for *Ivan Denisovitch. Inset* Jack Nicolson excites refined attention in hand-tailored evening wear and straggle

SMALL MATTERS OF GROOMING AND DEPORTMENT

to hippie, a bit to psychoanalysis and a lot to the parts they'd played. Not Shaving said – as well as Real Person and 'I'm not Hollywood' – that the Not Shaver didn't have to go to serious work that day, wasn't bound by Middle-American conventions (whatever these were supposed to be) and made no concessions to the publicity process. Interviews were an unwelcome intrusion on *a very private person*, a free man . . . not a star.

Not Shaving started, however, at almost precisely the time that most adult males in the Western world got access to constant hot water, aerosol shave foam and stainless-steel blades in dispensers. Actors started to look a whole lot more funky and *natural* about the same time people in the real world looked cleaner than ever. Their leisure-class convention of *authentic* and *sincere* was actually jet-set throwaway style or, to say the same thing, it was archaic.

Now Not Shaving has progressed to become an established fashion world accessory routine. One in three male models, in preposterously expensive Italian designer clothes, is Not Shaved. It's a statement, though, unlike the actors, you can't always work out exactly what they're saying.

Sometimes it's a bit sinister, sometimes a bit macho, but mainly its a bit Avant, post-punk. It suits the new unstructured clothing which, of course, is natural, *comfortable* and even, sometimes, politically conscious. Why shouldn't models be a bit deep? Why shouldn't a $750 Milano-Japanese cotton sports-style rig say something about the world we live in?

What it makes clear, however inadvertently, is that Not Shaving is simply a social style. If people who exist, professionally, simply to be seen and display clothes, who keep fit to within an inch of

Art Direction: A.W.A.
Photo: Denis Piel

their lives, never eat red meat and have their hair fixed by standby girls in the studio, if these guys don't shave then you *know* it's not about identifying with the people or being sincere or avoiding stardom or any of that thinking actor stuff. It's a big look like America primitive which appeals to folk who are neither American nor primitive.

Not Shaving; breaching the taboo, the purdah between clean-shaven and bearded has now

**Tessuti ETRO**

frontier of hairdressing in England which started with punk in 1976 and breached hundred-year conventions of which parts of your head hair should cover. Men and women had bits shaved off and other bits grown and dyed like Mohicans or Mr T. The dividing line between where hair should appear and where not, and which kind of hair was rude, just seemed to disappear.

Not Shaving, in that context, becomes just another option instead of a statement; it's no big thing. It doesn't say you're deep, or sincere, relate to the common person and used to love egg-creams in Brooklyn or any of the things thinking actors wish to say, but merely *look!*

Even on this level you can't see Not Shaving making a big contribution to Yuppie life – the ice-age professionals, running for their lives, in Neo-Classical kit (even in St Louis I *feel* I'm on Wall Street . . . ). Nor to those new freshmen who, we learn, are an even colder wave because they dream of Wall Street and IBM *now* and never have yearned for those Frye-booted freedom years their elder brothers went through. For them Not Shaving will look like the lovable old-fashioned gesture it is, made by people who grew up before the Oil War and the recession, AIDS and Ronald Reagan and fresh pasta to take out. *Period.*

The real stars of the young – MTV heroes like Boy George and Duran-Duran – do not go for the natural look favoured in easier times by stay cool, hang loose types – LA musicians and other residents of the old Hotel California. They are shaved and hairdone, flash and sharp, as true tribunes of the people always have been; for truly, the Not Shaving is a gesture of the romantic bourgeois. Boy George *always* shaves before applying make-up.

spread into a wider leisure class of creative types, starting of course with other films and TV folk. Twice this month already I've taken my cues from young Not Shaved TV directors wearing couturier mock-ups, of khaki army kit in one case, and jogging clothes in another. Creative types in advertising agencies go Not Shaved to meetings where their account people look as grey flannel as 1959.

Not Shaving, however, ties up with the new last

Early seventies
medium-low-market wally platform shoes
with interesting scalloped trim.
Note also trouser width

# P·L·A·T·F·O·R·M  B·O·O·T·S

You only have to say *platform boots* to mess up people's minds. It's like flares. The Big Leggy fashions of the early seventies, the last great pop time, are just so embarrassing; where were you in '72? On stilts with yards of polyester round your ankles? What a wally.

Who's the hopeless kid in *Saturday Night Fever* (1978), the one who falls off the bridge and dies? The one in the platforms, of course. And in Bill Forsyth's *Gregory's Girl* (1981), the loser's got platforms too. From 1976 to 1983 the last survivors were being teased out of the big legs look – wide trousers, big shoes, all that. *Everyone* knows you don't wear them anymore.

But platform boots *are* on the brain now; now the very last tramp, dwarf and recent Third World arrival is shot of them, now they've completely passed out of circulation like withdrawn coinage, and become a race memory. That's the time – and it's a golden rule established over nearly twenty years of fashion revivalism – that *those* people start taking an interest, looking them out in jumble sales, checking out who's got unsold *unused* warehouse stock. Now that there's no danger of confusion about the *statement* you're making (and the woman at the bus stop will just say 'I see they're bringing back those platform boots'), the plat-

forms, flares, big tie *Glam-Rock* revival that's been drifting about on the fringes for the last four years can get into higher gear.

It's May now and all the signs are there. Who's to say that there won't be at least one group costume and video that tugs at the Glam-Rock heartstrings, and one young designer who does a winter show featuring big platforms (like the New York man who went nap on the Eddie Sidgwick look this spring) by September? I'd lay money on it.

They really do get to you, platforms, because they were just about the last big *assertive* with-us-or-against-us mass fashion that filtered, tamed, into any shoe that acknowledged fashion at all. And, be honest, they looked wonderful and they felt wonderful – the Sex Stilts. A lot of relationships were ruined when people climbed off them at night. They solved problems for smaller types, of course, for here was elevation as legitimate fashion, and they stuck with the look as long as they could.

The look was all leg – long, wide, with a major statement at the bottom; the thick, heavy, bulky, inflexible, multi-coloured, appliquéd, late-pop, big shoe with big soles and chunky, clunky, thumping, lumpy, big heels. Not your Diana

Actress Sarah Miles kicks the platform
revival off in 1979. Note also
interesting print frock and crèche
shoulder-bag

Spencer look at all. Not your soft-shoe flat-foot
*ingénue* refinement. There were levels and levels
of Glam-Rock, of course, and different levels of
boots. Art Boots, a special from Chelsea Cobbler or
some such, could cost you over £80 even then –
and that really was money. But whatever the level,
it all looked extremely poppy, trashy, tacky and
thoroughly common. A rhinestone star from Saint
Laurent (unisex accessory) looked great because it
looked like about 50p's worth.

Glam-Rock was a major watershed. The beginning, for instance, of all the pop gender-bending
they've been on about since Dolly Boy George, for
Glam-Rock made some extremely coarse jokes
about all that. It was the beginning of ambiguity
and revivalism in pop music. At the same time it
was the last big, done-up, mass fashion look of the
kind that *seemed* – to outsiders at least – like a
total con done to working-class teens and tinies by
cynical manipulators; people you could imagine
being like Mike Mansfield in the control box at
'Supersonic', pressing the buttons for the flames
and dry ice. *Teenybopper* was an early seventies
word. For here were these kids looking more lurid,
hopeless and foolish than ever in clown-like get-
ups, listening to hod-carriers in lurex, like Slade or
Sweet, and freakish lumps like Gary Glitter. The
type of trimming culture critic who'd felt obliged
to write about pop culture from Beatlemania on,
usually felt safe to give Glam-Rock the go-by
altogether. Even the pretensions of David Bowie
and Bryan Ferry, who were popularly seen as part
of the same 'movement' at first, though they had
the art school chat, were largely ignored outside
fashionland and the music press. There wasn't
much in it in the way of *meaning*, was the verdict.

I loved it, of course. It wasn't just innate good
taste that drove me off platform boots. The scales
didn't fall from my eyes that quickly. It was
mainly falling over on the tube escalator. Re-

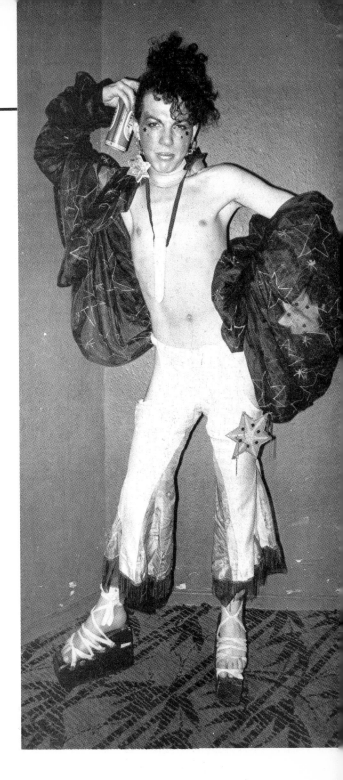

The Glam Rock revival mode: platform clogs, lurex and star motifs

nouncing them was really painful. I had three pairs; the first I wore with a pale blue, crimpy fabric New Cut wide-leg suit in 1971. It was fantastic. In Australia people came up in the street and asked you where you'd got the lot. After that I had a restrained brown pair, worn with subtle emerald green, front-pleated, wide-leg sailcloth trousers from Dandie Fashions on the King's Road, a blue one with a patch of snake. The problem was, by late 1972, that there were all these dreadful latecomers like Elton John and Queen and various Americans – more 'rock' types – who made you realise that the pop look really was totally charlie and you couldn't even wear the restrained tassel loafers on a small platform any more. A nice pair of soft leather correspondents was the thing.

The problem about reviving Glam-Rock is a kind of intellectual, even political, one however. The firsties who are doing it already with all the rhinestone and suchlike, say what they're doing is nothing like Glam-Rock which was – so they imply – so dumb, unsophisticated, non-liberated, non-eclectic and altogether old-world and authoritarian. This New Rococo is their own look. Post-pop, post-punk, post-everything. Any resemblance entirely coincidental. And, of course, they're right, the little snobs; it won't be any big thing again because people want more of a choice now.

But a resolutely unrefined Gary Glitter is forever hanging about, on to his fourth revival already, and early Glitter Band numbers like 'Leader of the Gang' and 'Rock and Roll Parts I and II' – thump, thump, thump go those boots – are recognised classics, endorsed by highbrows. The Sweet's 'Ballroom Blitz' and 'Teenage Rampage' are considered important texts in Midlands sociological circles. What's needed now is a documentary of the style – the Glittering Postures, so to speak, of the platform period.

PLATFORM BOOTS

## PHOTOGRAPH CREDITS

The author and publishers are grateful to the following for permission to reproduce photographs:
Pages 10–11 Andrew Stewart; 13 (left) Popperfoto; 13 (right) Rex Features; 14 (top) Universal Pictorial Press and Agency; 14 (bottom) John Sturrock/Network; 15 (top) Leslie Wong/Colorific; 15 (bottom) Steve Benbow/Colorific; 16 American Express; 18 John Swanell/*Daily Telegraph* Colour Library; 19 Laura Ashley; 20 Derry Moore; 21 Granada Television; 23 *Daily Express*; 27 Homer Sykes; 28 Cliff Jones/*The Kitchen and Bathroom Book* by Jose Manser, published by Pan Books; 31 Homer Sykes; 36 Andrew Stewart; 37 (top) Homer Sykes; 37 (bottom) Andrew Stewart; 40 Henry Grossman/*Daily Telegraph* Colour Library; 42 Rex Features; 44 John Downman/ Camerapix/Hutchison Library; 46 Tony Stone Associates; 47 (top) John Heseltine; 47 (bottom) Tony Stone Associates; 50 Tony Stone Associates; 53 Graham Attwood/*Harpers & Queen*; 54 Sotheby's; 55 (top) Jeremy Maas; 55 (bottom) Christie's; 58 Cecil Beaton/Camera Press; 60 Jeremy Maas; 61 Christie's; 62–67 Andrew Stewart; 68 and 69 (top) Peter Anderson; 69 (bottom) Allan Ballard/Scope Features; 71 Peter Anderson; 72 Patrick Hunt/Trevor Sorbie; 74 Eugene Adebari/Rex Features; 75 Rex Features; 78 Kobal Collection; 79 (left) Rex Features; 79 (right) Stephen Morley/David Redfern Library; 80 Duffy/*Sunday Times* Magazine; 81 Neil Matthews/Rex Features; 82 Kobal Collection; 84–85 Rex Features; 87–91 Judy Goldhill; 94 Rex Features; 95 Felici/ Gamma/F. Spooner; 96–7 (top) Rex Features; 96 (bottom) Universal Pictorial Press and Agency; 97 (bottom) Associated Newspapers Group ; 98 Rex Features; 99 Syndication International; 101 Pennie Smith; 102 Rex Features; 104–5 Elizabeth Whiting & Associates; 106 (left) Richard E. Aaron/David Redfern Library; 106–7 Rex Features; 108–9 Elizabeth Whiting & Associates; 114 Annie Leibovitz/Colorific; 116–17 Rex Features; 118 (left) Hovis Ltd; 118 (right) Collett, Dickenson, Pearce & Partners Ltd on behalf of Benson & Hedges Ltd; 119 (left) Linda McCartney; 119 (right) Kobal Collection; 121–5 Rex Features; 126 Syndication International; 127 Derek Ridgers.

Grateful thanks also to Astrohome, 47–49 Neal Street, London, WC2, and to Practical Styling, 16–18 St Giles High Street, London, WC2, for their co-operation.